"How do we encounter Scripture? Scripture is the living Word, and so we respond to it with the interpretive gifts given to us as readers, artists, and thinkers. *Drawing Near* makes creative response to the living Word a palpable, invitatory experience for all."

—**SALLY ITO**, adjunct English professor at Canadian Mennonite University and author of *Heart's Hydrography* and *The Emperor's Orphans*

"What a lovely thing: to reencounter resonant Bible narratives and blessings augmented by terrific creative imaginings. The Anabaptist artists and poets foregrounded in this volume, while invoking the productive reciprocity between visual art and poetry, suggest to us rich new ways to see and fresh ways to comprehend and remake what we've tended to embrace as familiar."

—**HILDI FROESE TIESSEN**, professor emerita of English and peace and conflict studies at Conrad Grebel University College

"This devotional book, with its intentionally chosen scripture passages, evocative art, and original poems by forty Anabaptist writers, suspends the reader in contemplation."

—**AILEEN FRIESEN**, associate professor and executive director of the Plett Foundation at University of Winnipeg

"For five centuries, the Anabaptist experience has been one of sturdy, deliberate, utilitarian application of our Christian faith. There has always been something practical and useful for us to do. But these five hundred years have also witnessed probing theological investigation, philosophical speculation, literary musing, and artistic imagination. The result has been a broadening of our collective experience and a deepening of our understanding of what it means to live a life of faith in the twenty-first century. *Drawing Near* is a welcome response to half a millennium of Anabaptist contemplation of the mysteries and verities that continue to enthrall, challenge, and inspire us."

—**HOWARD DYCK**, Canadian conductor and broadcaster

"The remarkable drawings and poems attractively curated in this devotional book shift the attention of Bible readers beyond the established and debated meanings of the biblical text to the trace of the divine voice in the ancient words of Scripture. While the visual art amplifies neglected details in key scripture passages, the poetry improvises startling new avenues of reflection that carry readers from the world of the Bible as envisioned in the drawings to the dramas and dilemmas of our own time. *Drawing Near* is a lively companion to the *Anabaptist Community Bible*, supplying provocative prompts for conversation in Bible study groups and startling sources of contemplation for personal spiritual renewal."

—**GERALD J. MAST**, professor of communication at Bluffton University

"Five hundred years ago, the Bible inspired a group of Christians to understand discipleship, love, and peace in new and exciting ways. Now as the heirs of Anabaptism celebrate their history, they also discover, through art and poetry, that the Bible continues as a living document. This book goes deep and invites readers to go deep also."

—**SHIRLEY HERSHEY SHOWALTER**, former professor and president of Goshen College and the cofounder of Grandmas for Love

"*Drawing Near* illustrates the power of ongoing revelation as the provocative art and poetry add new meaning and urgency to foundational scriptures."

—**ERVIN BECK**, professor emeritus of English at Goshen College

"I am not a poet—but poetry is a source of inspiration for me. I am not an artist—but art always accompanies my research for sermons. I love words and organize them into letters, simple cards to the unwell, and even into writing books. Wonderfully, the combination of scripture, poetry, and linocut art in this devotional will grab your imagination and draw you into the Spirit's tug toward justice, peace, and reconciliation."

—**DOROTHY NICKEL FRIESEN**, retired pastor and conference minister and author of *The Pastor Wears a Skirt*

"A reflective journal like no other, *Drawing Near* invites at once both *lectio divina* and *visio divina*—divine reading and divine seeing—throughout its page-by-page pattern of scripture passage, artist illustration, and poetry composed in response. Reflection prompts follow, with ample space for new words and images to appear, as the divine draws near in newly revelatory ways. A living prayer book for our time, *Drawing Near* is a complementary companion to the *Anabaptist Community Bible*."

—**ELIZABETH SCHMIDT**, pastor for congregational care at Bethel College Mennonite Church

DRAWING NEAR

DRAWING NEAR

A Devotional Journey with Art, Poetry, and Reflection

Edited by
Eileen R. Kinch and John D. Roth

HERALD
PRESS
Harrisonburg, Virginia

Herald Press
PO Box 866, Harrisonburg, Virginia 22803
www.HeraldPress.com

Library of Congress Cataloging-in-Publication Data
Names: Roth, John D., 1960- editor. | Kinch, Eileen R., 1981- editor.
Title: Drawing near : a devotional journey with art, poetry, and reflection / editors, John D. Roth, Eileen R. Kinch.
Description: Harrisonburg, Virginia : Herald Press, [2025]
Identifiers: LCCN 2024031474 (print) | LCCN 2024031475 (ebook) | ISBN 9781513815145 (hardcover) | ISBN 9781513815152 (ebook)
Subjects: LCSH: Christian art and symbolism—United States. | Christian poetry, American. | Anabaptists—United States. | Bible—Meditations. | Devotional exercises.
Classification: LCC BV153.U6 D83 2025 (print) | LCC BV153.U6 (ebook) | DDC 704.9/48--dc23/eng/20240828
LC record available at https://lccn.loc.gov/2024031474
LC ebook record available at https://lccn.loc.gov/2024031475

VERSA PRESS

Printing generously donated by Versa Press, East Peoria, IL
and Metamora Mennonite Church, Metamora, IL.

DRAWING NEAR

Library of Congress Control Number: 2024031474
International Standard Book Number: 978-1-5138-1514-5 (hardcover);
978-1-5138-1515-2 (ebook)
Printed in United States of America
Cover and interior design by Merrill Miller
Cover art by Dona Park

29 28 27 26 25 10 9 8 7 6 5 4 3 2 1

CONTENTS

PART 3: **FORGIVENESS, MEMORY, AND TRANSFORMATION**

PART 4: **RESISTANCE**

PART 5: **BONDAGE AND LIBERATION**

PART 8: **VISIONS OF THE FUTURE**

FOREWORD

IN 1755, THE TERM *anthology* referred to a collection of devotional pieces used by worshipers in the Greek Orthodox Church. That same year, Samuel Johnson published his *Dictionary of the English Language* and defined the word *anthology* as "a collection of flowers," an actual bouquet. Both senses of the word are useful in considering this thoughtfully arranged gathering of literary works—which is the contemporary meaning of the word *anthology*.

How is this book a bouquet? My guess is that some of the poets who happily contributed to this volume have never read a devotional book, let alone seen their work published in one. Others may write and read devotional literature regularly. Each of these poems is unique in tone and approach, each poet as different from the others as one flower of the field from the rest. And yet they are bound together in a single volume. Distinct and different works of literary art sprung from the impulse "To create. To begin again," as Abigail Carl-Klassen writes in her poem. Indeed, every work of art starts anew, even when it is occasioned by memories of the past.

The five hundredth anniversary of Anabaptism—marked by the first adult baptisms in Zurich, Switzerland, in 1525—prompted MennoMedia and its Anabaptism at 500 project to issue a new, illustrated study Bible. To give the commissioned artwork broader exposure and engage a wider range of readers, project director and editor John D. Roth conceived of the idea for this collection, enlisting Eileen R. Kinch to work closely with the texts and writers.

Notably, the Swiss Reformation, which shaped those first Anabaptists, was an iconoclastic movement. In response to the excesses of the Roman Catholic Church and local aristocracy, people destroyed or displaced paintings, sculptures, candlesticks, and musical instruments. They scraped frescoes from church walls or covered them with whitewash, insisting that the Word of God spoken in a local language was all that the faithful needed.

Yet lo and behold, the *Anabaptist Community Bible* comes with images! Poets of several generations who hold ties to Mennonite people or who themselves ascribe to Anabaptist values have written poems to accompany them! Is this anthology not a modest reminder that people can honor both individual difference and collective commitment at once? Is it not a small sign of hope that we can help to repair the violence of history?

And see what poetry can do. It can celebrate forgotten subversives, as in Carmen Susana Horst's poem for the clever Egyptian midwives Shiphrah and Puah. It can grieve, as in Ruth Ann Meyers Kulp's "Lament"; confess and dream, as in Dennis Huffman's "One Body"; and frame ambiguous praise, as in Patrick Friesen's "sons of water." Dramatic monologues speak miraculously from the point of view of another person in another time, as in the poems by Shari Miller Wagner and Keith Ratzlaff. Poetry can both attend to this world and imagine it transformed, as in Sarah Kinsel's "You are like trees planted by streams of water" and Jesse Nathan's "Stone of Help," which sees even to the "end of suffering." Behold all pleasures this book contains.

—Julia Spicher Kasdorf
Poet, essayist, editor, director of Creative Writing, and Liberal Arts professor of English at Penn State University

INTRODUCTION

YOU HOLD IN YOUR HANDS A UNIQUE VOLUME. *Drawing Near* is a devotional book that engages scripture passages through art images, but it is also an experiment in ekphrasis, or writing poems in response to art, thereby creating a literary collection of poetry by forty Anabaptist-related authors. The devotional invites you to pause, to reflect, and to attend closely to the biblical text through art, poetry, and contemplation.

Drawing Near is a companion volume to the *Anabaptist Community Bible*, part of the Anabaptism at 500 anniversary project by MennoMedia. When poet Julia Kasdorf and Anabaptism at 500 project director John D. Roth asked me to consider being part of this project, it did not occur to me to say no. Some Anabaptists feel a call to making art and writing poems as faithful responses to Christ's claim on their lives. Honoring and encouraging this faithfulness seemed like a good opportunity for a fresh encounter with the living God.

Since the tendency of many study Bibles is to focus on the life of the mind, the editors of this devotional sought to highlight the artwork that had been commissioned for the *Anabaptist Community Bible* while also honoring other creative community expressions of identity and faith. The forty Anabaptist poets who contributed to this volume reflect that goal in a significant way.

Together with Julia Kasdorf and fellow poets Jeff Gundy and Ann Hostetler, John Roth and I formed a list of poets who might contribute to this project. We are grateful to each of the poets who said yes.

The collection of poems in *Drawing Near* ranges widely, both in form and content. Some are formal with deliberate use of rhyme and meter; many are free-form. In this volume, we see senryu, iambic pentameter, shape poetry, a sonnet, a compressed lyric essay, and a list poem. Some poems are reverent meditations; others openly question. Some poems focus more on the artwork; others focus on the scripture passage. But all poems creatively engage the biblical text and offer evidence of "drawing near" to the themes of the scripture and art.

In contrast to the early Swiss Brethren, who tended to emphasize the outer, or literal, word of Scripture, other Anabaptists emphasized the inner word—a Spirit-infused meaning of Scripture. *Drawing Near* leans on this tradition.

Each of the forty devotional entries includes a scripture passage, an art image in linocut style, a poem, and several questions for reflection. We have divided the poems into eight thematic units, suggesting a devotional rhythm in which you reflect on five passages, poems, and images each week. As you spend time with each of these offerings, we invite you to listen for the inner word of God. What does the scripture text evoke in you? How does the artwork reflect the passage? How does the poem engage the passage? Does a poem or passage inspire you? Unsettle you? Offend you? We invite you to ask yourself why.

Each entry includes space for you to respond with reflections, a prayer, a sketch of your own, or even a poem. As you ruminate on these images and texts, allow yourself to enter into a conversation with Scripture that touches your spirit.

Ponder. Attend. Gaze. Draw near. The inner word of God is never far away.

—Eileen R. Kinch, poetry editor

PART 1

God's Shalom Order

CREATION CARE

READ: GENESIS 1:26–31

Then God said, "Let us make humanity in our image to resemble us so that they may take charge of the fish of the sea, the birds in the sky, the livestock, all the earth, and all the crawling things on earth."

God created humanity in God's own image,
in the divine image God created them,
male and female God created them.

God blessed them and said to them, "Be fertile and multiply; fill the earth and master it. Take charge of the fish of the sea, the birds in the sky, and everything crawling on the ground." Then God said, "I now give to you all the plants on the earth that yield seeds and all the trees whose fruit produces its seeds within it. These will be your food. To all wildlife, to all the birds in the sky, and to everything crawling on the ground—to everything that breathes—I give all the green grasses for food." And that's what happened. God saw everything he had made: it was supremely good.

Creation Care DONA PARK

Signs for Sacred Times

Let us gather again, together in one
Place. In the land covered and uncovered

By the waters moved by the breath of God.
Let us wonder at the signs to mark the sacred

Times. The lights: for seasons, for days, for years.
The beasts and the birds and the trees and

The seeds. And the creatures that move
Along the earth. And the fruit from the tree

With the seed. And the seed within. And the land
And the water and the breath that moves

To create. To begin again. The evening
And the morning—the first day.

—Abigail Carl-Klassen

FOR REFLECTION:

- Take some time to meditate on the artwork. Are your eyes drawn first to Adam and Eve or to the birds hiding in the tree?
- Note how the poem uses repetition, usually with the word *the* or *and* preceding the next image. How does the repetition build as you read the poem?
- What is the role of breath in the poem, whether God's or your own, when reading it?
- What is the "seed within" you right now that yearns to participate with the breath of God in creation?

LOVE THE LORD YOUR GOD

READ: DEUTERONOMY 6:4–9

Israel, listen! Our God is the LORD! Only the LORD!

Love the LORD your God with all your heart, all your being, and all your strength. These words that I am commanding you today must always be on your minds. Recite them to your children. Talk about them when you are sitting around your house and when you are out and about, when you are lying down and when you are getting up. Tie them on your hand as a sign. They should be on your forehead as a symbol. Write them on your house's doorframes and on your city's gates.

Love the Lord Your God DONA PARK

Shema

When we say this is our God,
which do we mean:
angel who wounded Jacob,
silence after the storm,
bloody body on a tree?

This woman in a field of water,
peace above her head,
sun and moon together,
the curve of breasts
as close as breath—

see, she is waiting.

Is this God, or my mother, telling me?
Is this the unfurling of my own divinity?

Hear, O Israel, you who struggle with God.
The LORD is one. She contains all things.
She leans but is not unsteady.
Around her plants are growing.

Listen, it's been like this from the beginning.
Not so much rules but instructions:
how to make the world and love it,
how to be one with whatever comes,
rock and wind and cloud,
how to stay still in the swirling.

YHWH: the sound of one woman breathing.

—Anita Hooley Yoder

FOR REFLECTION:

- The image created by artist Dona Park in response to the Shema—a prayer central to Judaism—is infused with layers of meaning. What captures your attention first? What do you notice upon further reflection?

- The poem that accompanies the artwork and text concludes with the tetragrammaton, a combination of four Hebrew letters that form the ancient Hebrew name of God, YHWH. Then follows an evocative phrase reminiscent of the famous Japanese Zen koan "the sound of one hand clapping." Reflect for a time on this phrase as you look at the image. Then read the scripture text once more.

- Share your thoughts in the space below.

WHAT DOES THE LORD REQUIRE?

READ: MICAH 6:6–8

With what should I approach the LORD
 and bow down before God on high?
Should I come before him with entirely burned offerings,
 with year-old calves?
Will the LORD be pleased with thousands of rams,
 with many torrents of oil?
Should I give my oldest child for my crime;
 the fruit of my body for the sin of my spirit?
He has told you, human one, what is good and
 what the LORD requires from you:
  to do justice, embrace faithful love, and walk humbly with your God.

What Does the Lord Require? SARAH FULLER

We Are Sunflowers

What is good?
To stand in color, against the pallid sky:
Hummingbird purple, beetroot red,
solar flare yellow. We are flames
that flutter and twist and spike the air
with playfulness and rage.
What does our God require of us?
To plant our feet in the mud of this magnetic garden
from which we can sprout, blossom,
become.

Humility is crisp, not soft
not broken, not small. It stands
at full height, unflinching and ready
a head above the other stalks, a beacon
of uncomplicated light.

As the evening sun melts into a striptease
casting off her familiar orange and slipping
into a luminescent robe
she dances with the nameless hues
connecting points of light between black,
brown, gold, magenta, and midnight.
In darkness, we wait.

Mercy is the morning rain
masked and delirious, a silver drum
rumbling its petition. And justice,
that long-beaked bird, awakens us
with frenetic humming
burrows all the way into our succulent center
nagging at the interior walls
loosening, tugging, prying, undoing.
What does this moment require of us?
A freestanding disarray, a quiet decomposition.

Even as the predatory wind wears us down
and night creatures hollow out our inflorescence,
nectar drips and hungry seeds fall to the ground.

—Jessica Smucker

FOR REFLECTION:

- “We Are Sunflowers” is a fine example of an ekphrastic poem—a poem that begins with an image, typically a work of art, and then offers an imaginative narrative that amplifies or expands its meaning.

- Christians who are familiar with the Micah 6 scripture passage are likely to associate it with discipleship or the language of ethics. Yet this ekphrastic poem responds to the artwork by posing a different set of images and questions. How does the rich, descriptive language of hummingbirds, mud, the evening sun, and the morning rain change how you think about these verses?

- The poet asks, “What does this moment require of us?” How do you respond? What images or words resonate with you?

THE YEAR OF JUBILEE

READ: LEVITICUS 25:1–13, 35–38

The LORD said to Moses on Mount Sinai, Speak to the Israelites and say to them: Once you enter the land that I am giving you, the land must celebrate a sabbath rest to the LORD. You will plant your fields for six years, and prune your vineyards and gather their crops for six years. But in the seventh year the land will have a special sabbath rest, a Sabbath to the LORD: You must not plant your fields or prune your vineyards. You must not harvest the secondary growth of your produce or gather the grapes of your freely growing vines. It will be a year of special rest for the land. Whatever the land produces during its sabbath will be your food—for you, for your male and female servants, and for your hired laborers and foreign guests who live with you, as well as for your livestock and for the wild animals in your land. All of the land's produce can be eaten.

Count off seven weeks of years—that is, seven times seven—so that the seven weeks of years totals forty-nine years. Then have the trumpet blown on the tenth day of the seventh month. Have the trumpet blown throughout your land on the Day of Reconciliation. You will make the fiftieth year holy, proclaiming freedom throughout the land to all its inhabitants. It will be a Jubilee year for you: each of you must return to your family property and to your extended family. The fiftieth year will be a Jubilee year for you. Do not plant, do not harvest the secondary growth, and do not gather from the freely growing vines because it is a Jubilee: it will be holy to you. You can eat only the produce directly out of the field. Each of you must return to your family property in this year of Jubilee. . . .

If one of your fellow Israelites faces financial difficulty and is in a shaky situation with you, you must assist them as you would an immigrant or foreign guest so that they can survive among you. Do not take interest from them, or any kind of profit from interest, but fear your God so that your fellow Israelite can survive among you. Do not lend a poor Israelite money with interest or lend food at a profit. I am the LORD your God, who brought you out from the land of Egypt to give you Canaan's land and to be your God.

The Year of Jubilee SARAH FULLER

La Milagrosa Canyon

Ask the canyon—there is a day set
for returning home. Down the granite slopes
and over every ledge, water will seek

a path out, a path on. Through the long wait,
wildflowers kindle and fade, saguaros blossom
into crimson fruit, tortoises sleep through winter

and emerge to quiet life. All our work
belongs to God, all our being. Little heart,
can you bear the water continuing

to pare down rock, to loose what has been bound
and bring you to yourself again, changed? Birdsong
and all the clamor of the city just beyond here

are passing through. Return, like the liquid
trill descending from the wren that stays
unseen. Bless every silence you cannot keep.

—Julie Swarstad Johnson

FOR REFLECTION:

- In Leviticus 25, the Israelites are instructed to allow their land to remain fallow every seventh year. After seven cycles of seven years, they are to practice a year of Jubilee in which debts are forgiven, those who are enslaved are set free, and property is returned to the original owners. "There is a day set," the poet suggests, "for returning home." What does this mean for you? How have you experienced Jubilee?

- What other forms of liberation—what kind of transformation—do you see suggested in the poem? What resonates within you?

LOVING YOUR NEIGHBOR

READ: LUKE 10:25–37

A legal expert stood up to test Jesus. "Teacher," he said, "what must I do to gain eternal life?"

Jesus replied, "What is written in the Law? How do you interpret it?"

He responded, "You must love the Lord your God with all your heart, with all your being, with all your strength, and with all your mind, and love your neighbor as yourself."

Jesus said to him, "You have answered correctly. Do this and you will live."

But the legal expert wanted to prove that he was right, so he said to Jesus, "And who is my neighbor?"

Jesus replied, "A man went down from Jerusalem to Jericho. He encountered thieves, who stripped him naked, beat him up, and left him near death. Now it just so happened that a priest was also going down the same road. When he saw the injured man, he crossed over to the other side of the road and went on his way. Likewise, a Levite came by that spot, saw the injured man, and crossed over to the other side of the road and went on his way. A Samaritan, who was on a journey, came to where the man was. But when he saw him, he was moved with compassion. The Samaritan went to him and bandaged his wounds, tending them with oil and wine. Then he placed the wounded man on his own donkey, took him to an inn, and took care of him. The next day, he took two full days' worth of wages and gave them to the innkeeper. He said, 'Take care of him, and when I return, I will pay you back for any additional costs.' What do you think? Which one of these three was a neighbor to the man who encountered thieves?"

Then the legal expert said, "The one who demonstrated mercy toward him."

Jesus told him, "Go and do likewise."

Loving Your Neighbor DONA PARK

At Dusk a Merchant

At dusk a merchant
stumbling down the bloody way
from temple to the site
of fallen walls and slaughter
was ambushed, beaten, left
for dead. Then came the scavengers:
first passed the one who, praising
heaven, tore from the body grace
to not have been this poor unfortunate;
then circled by a second who wrought beautiful,
holy laments from other's anguish.
A third, seeing a fellow traveler,
stopped, dressed their wounds,
and carried them to shelter.

The flustered innkeeper frowned
at the shivering heap
curled like a street dog
on the merchant's mat,
rubbed the silver coins
placed on the counter.
And where will you be?
I must head back across the river
before dawn, or I'll be killed.

The keeper, considering
the merchant's accent,
wondered if he should seek
a lawyer for advice on liability,
but, considering the time of day,
the cost of paying overtime,
the cost of living,
the cash in hand,
the price of mercy,
he relented.

That night
wrapped in time-torn shawls
and huddled on the stone-cold step
outside the door,
the keeper watched as clouds
were swept away, unveiling
bright-starred heavens,
clearing his anxious mind,
and, for the first time felt,
after a long and troubled life,
peace.

—David Waltner-Toews

FOR REFLECTION:

- The story of the good Samaritan includes at least six main actors—the traveler, a shadowy group of thieves, a priest, a Levite, the Samaritan who tends to the traveler, and the innkeeper. The poem retells the story focusing on the perspective of the innkeeper. As you read the scripture passage, which character stands out most clearly in your mind? Why? Read the story and poem again . . . and then again, each time consciously focusing on a different character.

- Consider writing a poem from the perspective of a different character in the story.

PART 2

Suffering and Grief

WHEN YOU PASS THROUGH THE WATERS

READ: ISAIAH 43:1–4

But now, says the LORD—
the one who created you, Jacob,
  the one who formed you, Israel:
Don't fear, for I have redeemed you;
  I have called you by name; you are mine.
When you pass through the waters, I will be with you;
  when through the rivers, they won't sweep over you.
When you walk through the fire, you won't be scorched
  and flame won't burn you.
I am the LORD your God,
  the holy one of Israel, your savior.
I have given Egypt as your ransom,
  Cush and Seba in your place.
Because you are precious in my eyes,
  you are honored, and I love you.
I give people in your place,
  and nations in exchange for your life.

When You Pass through the Waters DONA PARK

Passing through Waters, or Visit to Switzerland

I didn't know what to do but smile
for the photo with the Kreuzgasse street sign
over my head marking where Anabaptists
received their judgment, or next to the plaque
identifying how Felix Manz drowned. The water
of the Limmat River was so clear
the pebbles at the river's bottom sparkled with sunlight.
Did Felix ask as he passed through this river,
that it would not sweep over him?
Did others pray when they walked through fire,
that they would not burn? It would be nice
if life was as easy as a stroll along Lake Zurich
in June, with the statue of Ganymede looking over
sailboats and swans. There are days
when water fills the lungs
and skin gets singed, even for those of us
without the credentials to be honored in the *Martyrs Mirror*.
Sometimes it must be enough
that it is written "Do not fear," that it is written
"I am with you," that it is written
"I am the Lord your God." Sometimes the words
scoop us up from the raging waters and hold us
as if in the palms of God's hands.

—Debra Gingerich

FOR REFLECTION:

- As you reflect on the verses from Isaiah and contemplate the artwork, allow yourself to recall times when you have experienced the certainty of being "called by name" and known the assurance of God's loving embrace.

- The poem raises a haunting question: Is God still present when the waters overwhelm us and the fire rages? What form has that presence taken for you? Consider writing a poem in response.

JERUSALEM'S SUFFERING

READ: LAMENTATIONS 1:1–2, 20–22

Oh, no!
She sits alone, the city that was once full of people.
Once great among nations, she has become like a widow.
Once a queen over provinces, she has become a slave.

She weeps bitterly in the night, her tears on her cheek.
None of her lovers comfort her.
    All her friends lied to her; they have become her enemies.

. . . .

Pay attention, LORD, for I am in trouble. My stomach is churning;
my heart is pounding inside me because I am so bitter.
In the streets the sword kills; in the house it is like death.

People heard that I was groaning, that I had no comforter.
All my enemies heard about my distress; they were thrilled that you had done this.
Bring the day you have announced so they become like me!

Let all their evil come before you.
Then injure them like you've injured me because of all my wrong acts;
my groans are many, my heart is sick.

Jerusalem's Suffering LISA OBIREK

Lament

I sit in the shade,
a circle of quiet,

shaken by loss
of family, and friends,
homes, and futures,

the skin of my forearms
a backsplash for tears,
knees bruised from many
long nights of pleading.

No sheltering trees
to comfort, sustain,

no traveling rivers
to carry me away
from the darkness of pain,

only clouds to embrace
the smoke drifting up
from my smoldering grief.

Can the bones of my
forebears call forth
the memory, the mercy
of Love everlasting?

I sit in the shade,
a circle of quiet,

head bowed, spirit breath,
my whole body
still

waiting.

—Ruth Ann Meyers Kulp

FOR REFLECTION:

- All of us have experienced loss—the loss of a loved one, the loss of a relationship, the loss of a dream, and maybe even the loss of hope. The book of Lamentations names the human reality of loss without any sugarcoating. As you read the text, gaze at the image, and reflect on the poem, allow yourself time to sit with your lament—to name the losses, to grieve the disappointments. Where is your "shade, / a circle of quiet"?

- What has enabled you to make it through the proverbial valley of the shadow of death? Where have you found solace or comfort?

- Reflect on the final verse of the biblical text (Lamentations 1:22). How do you react to the writer's appeal for God's vengeance on those who have caused pain?

JONAH BALKS AT GOD'S MERCY

READ: JONAH 4:1–11

But Jonah thought this was utterly wrong, and he became angry. He prayed to the LORD, "Come on, LORD! Wasn't this precisely my point when I was back in my own land? This is why I fled to Tarshish earlier! I know that you are a merciful and compassionate God, very patient, full of faithful love, and willing not to destroy. At this point, LORD, you may as well take my life from me, because it would be better for me to die than to live."

The LORD responded, "Is your anger a good thing?" But Jonah went out from the city and sat down east of the city. There he made himself a hut and sat under it, in the shade, to see what would happen to the city.

Then the LORD God provided a shrub, and it grew up over Jonah, providing shade for his head and saving him from his misery. Jonah was very happy about the shrub. But God provided a worm the next day at dawn, and it attacked the shrub so that it died. Then as the sun rose God provided a dry east wind, and the sun beat down on Jonah's head so that he became faint. He begged that he might die, saying, "It's better for me to die than to live."

God said to Jonah, "Is your anger about the shrub a good thing?"

Jonah said, "Yes, my anger is good—even to the point of death!"

But the LORD said, "You 'pitied' the shrub, for which you didn't work and which you didn't raise; it grew in a night and perished in a night. Yet for my part, can't I pity Nineveh, that great city, in which there are more than one hundred twenty thousand people who can't tell their right hand from their left, and also many animals?"

Jonah Balks at God's Mercy MATTHEW REGIER

Jonah and the Vine

How could I ever hide from you?
Is it because I am afraid?
                                        I'm afraid all the time.
As the sun breaks my skin, I cry out to you.
Aren't my tears enough for you? My prayers?
When I told the sailors,
                                        This is my fault—let me go to the storm,
and they threw me to the dark waters
of your truest lessons,
and I prayed for the calm, asked for your forgiveness
for my running away from you,
                                        the shelter you sent—the great fish—
                                        was the size of my fear,
and in the warm chamber of its belly,
I was safe. Outside this awful city,
I could not even rest.
The sun was cruel and mocked me.
                                        All I had was this modest vine—
                                        standing tall, hovering over me, protectively,
and I could finally close my eyes
after this difficult journey for you.
Under the vine, I wondered,
Why not punish this city?
Their repenting comes too little, too late—
But as soon as this thought blazed
across my mind's eye,
so, too, did the sun once more,
                                        as the vine had suddenly disappeared!
The scorching east wind cut into my skin,
as I realized my mistake—
questioning your mercy, your patience.
                                Oh, Lord, how I am sorry!

—Shannon McKeehen

FOR REFLECTION:

- As you read the text and reflect on the image and poem, where do you see Jonah? On the ship in a storm? In the belly of the whale? Arguing with God? Under the shadow of the shrub tree? Where do you see yourself in this story?

- This poem splits words into two columns. How does this affect the way you read the poem?

- Write a poem in response to this story. Consider splitting your poem into columns or even between different voices. What seems important to put in one column or another?

THE TRAVAILS OF JOB

READ: JOB 3:1–10

Afterward, Job spoke up and cursed the day he was born.

> Job said:
> Perish the day I was born,
>   the night someone said,
>   "A boy has been conceived."
> That day—let it be darkness;
>   may God above ignore it,
>   and light not shine on it.
> May deepest darkness claim it
>   and a cloud linger over it;
>   may all that darkens the day terrify it.
> May gloom seize that night;
>   may it not be counted in the days of a year;
>   may it not appear in the months.
> May that night be childless;
>   may no happy singing come in it.
> May those who curse the day curse it,
>   those with enough skill to awaken Leviathan.
> May its evening stars stay dark;
>   may it wait in vain for light;
>   may it not see dawn's gleam,
>   because it didn't close the doors of my mother's womb,
>   didn't hide trouble from my eyes.

The Travails of Job RANDY HORST

What Remains

When grief goes on
despite abundant blessings
the surface might imply a kind of peace
that takes replacements as an equal measure
to what was lost.

But underneath
remains the bitter prologue
where everything was snatched away at once.
What does it take to see a faith unravel
this side of death?

And next there comes
a life of unforgetting
where give and take can strike at any time;
and lips that dare to speak a proper blessing
might rather curse.

But nothing said
is better still in answer
to One who neither caused nor calmed the grief;
a silence in the storm. A breath enduring.
A thread of faith.

—*Adam M. L. Tice*

FOR REFLECTION:

- The story of Job raises the timeless question of innocent suffering. "What does it take," the poet asks, "to see a faith unravel / this side of death?" List several moments in your life when you can relate to the suffering of Job—maybe not in the same detail, but with the same emotional and spiritual sense of desolation and meaninglessness.

- For some people, these moments become occasions where faith is strengthened; others experience it as an "unraveling." How have you responded?

- What counsel, if any, do you have for family and friends who experience similar suffering? How would you express it in a poem?

THE WOMAN WITH A HEMORRHAGE

READ: MARK 5:24–34

A swarm of people were following Jesus, crowding in on him. A woman was there who had been bleeding for twelve years. She had suffered a lot under the care of many doctors, and had spent everything she had without getting any better. In fact, she had gotten worse. Because she had heard about Jesus, she came up behind him in the crowd and touched his clothes. She was thinking, If I can just touch his clothes, I'll be healed. Her bleeding stopped immediately, and she sensed in her body that her illness had been healed.

At that very moment, Jesus recognized that power had gone out from him. He turned around in the crowd and said, "Who touched my clothes?"

His disciples said to him, "Don't you see the crowd pressing against you? Yet you ask, 'Who touched me?'" But Jesus looked around carefully to see who had done it.

The woman, full of fear and trembling, came forward. Knowing what had happened to her, she fell down in front of Jesus and told him the whole truth. He responded, "Daughter, your faith has healed you; go in peace, healed from your disease."

The Woman with a Hemorrhage SARAH FULLER

Flowing (Luke 8:43–48)

Her face drained—
like an empty vessel she stands,
one hand hidden in shame
as the blood flow of twelve years
burns like a flame,
searing in its pain.

Yet she finds the courage
to fling the other hand, palm open,
into a stream overflowing its vessel,
swirling beside and above her,
cascading like endless grace,
surrounding her feet and
flowing into the beyond.

As she poises on the edge of hope,
a fully formed butterfly hovers
before taking flight
on faith.

—Esther Yoder Stenson

FOR REFLECTION:

- This familiar story describes a woman who has suffered from a chronic health issue, has desperately sought the counsel of multiple doctors, and is now impoverished by medical bills. She is poised, as the poet suggests, "on the edge of hope." Reflect on a time that you experienced a sense of physical, emotional, social, or financial hopelessness. Where have you found hope?

- Have you witnessed a "fully formed butterfly" in the midst of a crisis? If so, what form did it take? Consider writing a poem or prayer.

PART 3

Forgiveness, Memory, and Transformation

ESAU FORGIVES JACOB

READ: GENESIS 33:1–11

Jacob looked up and saw Esau approaching with four hundred men. Jacob divided the children among Leah, Rachel, and the two women servants. He put the servants and their children first, Leah and her children after them, and Rachel and Joseph last. He himself went in front of them and bowed to the ground seven times as he was approaching his brother. But Esau ran to meet him, threw his arms around his neck, kissed him, and they wept. Esau looked up and saw the women and children and said, "Who are these with you?"

Jacob said, "The children that God generously gave your servant." The women servants and their children came forward and bowed down. Then Leah and her servants also came forward and bowed, and afterward Joseph and Rachel came forward and bowed.

Esau said, "What's the meaning of this entire group of animals that I met?"

Jacob said, "To ask for my master's kindness."

Esau said, "I already have plenty, my brother. Keep what's yours."

Jacob said, "No, please, do me the kindness of accepting my gift. Seeing your face is like seeing God's face, since you've accepted me so warmly. Take this present that I've brought because God has been generous to me, and I have everything I need." So Jacob persuaded him, and he took it.

Esau Forgives Jacob SARAH FULLER

Jacob and Esau: The Embrace

The heavenly being softens the sky
with her feathers and tears, shimmers
the light with her tail. The date tree crescendos
leafy hallelujahs and ripens sweet joy,
as Esau wraps his hairy arms around his brother.

But in the womb, they jostled as two nations,
a prophecy given to their mother:
the older will serve the younger.

The firstborn red and hairy like a garment,
Jacob grasping Esau's heel as they leave the womb.

Everything doomed,
a stolen birthright, a hijacked blessing,
a murderous grudge.

So many woolly tricks,
decades wallowing in hatred, seeking riches and wives.
So easy to forget Jacob comes with gifts to meet Esau,
bows to the ground seven times,
to forget how they weep,
how Jacob sees the face of God in his brother.

Perhaps they hear the fragrant song of forgiveness
bursting from the earth.
    Listen.

—*Cheryl Denise*

FOR REFLECTION:

- Although our hearts may rejoice when we witness the embrace of former enemies, we know that reconciliation is always more complicated than a hug. What will it take for the relationship between Jacob and Esau to be truly repaired? What, as the poem asks, is the role of memory in reconciliation?

- When have you heard "the fragrant song of forgiveness / bursting from the earth"? Through which senses—sight, sound, smell, touch, taste—have you perceived it?

- Write or sketch your response in the space below.

THE EBENEZER STONE

READ: 1 SAMUEL 7:7–12

When the Philistines heard that the Israelites had assembled at Mizpah, the Philistine rulers went up to attack Israel. When the Israelites learned of this, they were afraid of the Philistines. The Israelites said to Samuel, "Please don't stop praying to the LORD our God for us, so God will save us from the Philistines' power!" So Samuel took a suckling lamb and offered it as an entirely burned offering to the LORD. Samuel cried out in prayer to the LORD for Israel, and the LORD answered him.

While Samuel was offering the entirely burned offering, the Philistines advanced to attack Israel. But the LORD thundered against the Philistines with a great blast on that very day, throwing the Philistines into such a panic that they were defeated by Israel. The Israelite soldiers came out of Mizpah and pursued the Philistines. They struck them down until they reached a place just below Beth-car. Then Samuel took a stone and set it up between Mizpah and Jeshanah. He named it Ebenezer, explaining, "The LORD helped us to this very point."

The Ebenezer Stone MATTHEW REGIER

Stone of Help

Let it stand for the end of it.
Let it stand also for a Lord
who does the battling so the people
themselves do not become butchers.
Let it stand for a thunder
and a thunder's after-whisper
and the after-whisper of a rainy wind.
Let no more names be unhinged
by its honor. Rough marker on the soil
let it stand for the imagination of suffering.
Stand for the end of the suffering
it stands for, and all the posturing
so that even the story of itself
is only a sign of a cold new wonder.

—Jesse Nathan

FOR REFLECTION:

- Humans—individually and collectively—generally have poor memories; we are quick to forget what matters most. Thus, at various times in the Old Testament, the children of Israel set up markers or monuments to help them remember stories of God's miraculous intervention at vulnerable moments. How do you remember formative moments in the development of your character or spirit?
- Do you have any Ebenezer stones in your life? What physical objects help you remember who you are (or who you want to be)?
- Monuments, the poet reminds us, are often erected to honor war heroes. What would a monument designed to "stand for the end of suffering" look like? Sketch some possibilities in the space below.

LOVING ENEMIES

READ: MATTHEW 5:43–48

You have heard that it was said, You must love your neighbor and hate your enemy. But I say to you, love your enemies and pray for those who harass you so that you will be acting as children of your Father who is in heaven. He makes the sun rise on both the evil and the good and sends rain on both the righteous and the unrighteous. If you love only those who love you, what reward do you have? Don't even the tax collectors do the same? And if you greet only your brothers and sisters, what more are you doing? Don't even the Gentiles do the same? Therefore, just as your heavenly Father is complete in showing love to everyone, so also you must be complete.

Loving Enemies SARAH FULLER

But I Say to You

Heaven weeps
on the just and unjust, waters dividing
into worlds above. Below,
the earth breathes. Let there be.
Bleeding heart, a sword
will pierce yours also. First
that he loved. Form a fist. Raise it.
Release. As it is on earth. Stay
your sword, this is heaven's body
dividing, a love to spare
for sparrows. Broken,
the dark leaves. Do not resist
rebirth. The earth groans. Sky seeps
into furrows. In secret:
wings, a formation. This is love
unfurling.

—Angeline Schellenberg

FOR REFLECTION:

- Christians throughout the ages have both exalted in these words of Jesus and struggled to make sense of them, especially in circumstances of tyranny or abuse. Reflect on the evocative image for several minutes with the words of Jesus echoing in your mind.

- Reread the poem. Sit for another moment with the art and poetry.

- What is the Spirit stirring in your heart? What words rise?

EMMAUS ROAD: BREAKING BREAD

READ: LUKE 24:13–33

On that same day, two disciples were traveling to a village called Emmaus, about seven miles from Jerusalem. They were talking to each other about everything that had happened. While they were discussing these things, Jesus himself arrived and joined them on their journey. They were prevented from recognizing him.

He said to them, "What are you talking about as you walk along?" They stopped, their faces downcast.

The one named Cleopas replied, "Are you the only visitor to Jerusalem who is unaware of the things that have taken place there over the last few days?"

He said to them, "What things?"

They said to him, "The things about Jesus of Nazareth. Because of his powerful deeds and words, he was recognized by God and all the people as a prophet. But our chief priests and our leaders handed him over to be sentenced to death, and they crucified him. We had hoped he was the one who would redeem Israel. All these things happened three days ago. But there's more: Some women from our group have left us stunned. They went to the tomb early this morning and didn't find his body. They came to us saying that they had even seen a vision of angels who told them he is alive. Some of those who were with us went to the tomb and found things just as the women said. They didn't see him."

Then Jesus said to them, "You foolish people! Your dull minds keep you from believing all that the prophets talked about. Wasn't it necessary for the Christ to suffer these things and then enter into his glory?" Then he interpreted for them the things written about himself in all the scriptures, starting with Moses and going through all the Prophets.

When they came to Emmaus, he acted as if he was going on ahead. But they urged him, saying, "Stay with us. It's nearly evening, and the day is almost over." So he went in to stay with them. After he took his seat at the table with them, he took the bread, blessed and broke it, and gave it to them. Their eyes were opened and they recognized him, but he disappeared from their sight. They said to each other, "Weren't our hearts on fire when he spoke to us along the road and when he explained the scriptures for us?"

They got up right then and returned to Jerusalem. They found the eleven and their companions gathered together.

Emmaus Road: Breaking Bread MATTHEW REGIER

What the Artist Knows about Bread and Belief

How, in a few moments, bread will fall to the table
and these two will see only one another and broken
scattered crumbs.

How a maker can sometimes etch wonder into linotype, show
the breathtaken body's impulse to press a hand to the breast
bone, the singed heart stopping and starting again?

How does the pulped or woven paper feel beneath a fingertip scanning
a text for a word, exact? How do we explain longing and loss,
how when everything becomes clear you cannot help but ask:

Were not our own hearts?
Were not our own minds?
How empty were our hollowed-out hands?

Each time a savior appears a disappearance seems to follow.
These stunned ones might also hope to mist into mere spirit
and evaporate from the world.

But the artist knows in a few more moments they will turn
toward the window's arch in a gesture like recollection
and glimpse a familiar rutted road they walked to get here.

Wanderer, whispers a Spirit in the room, dwelling not in ether but in breath,
you come to taste and tell the truth with your very lips.
Take the woodcut way that turns and crooks, feel

the earth's grooves beneath you, the bread inside you, as you make a path
towards astonishment, towards an exact word you might barely believe
yet, on your tongue, might say.

—David C. Wright

FOR REFLECTION:

- In this ekphrastic poem, the poet invites us to ponder the image with some specific cues, urging us to pay attention to gestures, emotions, and insights that the scripture and image seem to capture. Do you see in the image what the poet sees? What else stirs your heart and your imagination?

- What does this poem say about art and the artistic process? Where have you sensed God in your process of creating?

LYDIA'S CONVERSION

READ: ACTS 16:13–15

On the Sabbath we went outside the city gate to the riverbank, where we thought there might be a place for prayer. We sat down and began to talk with the women who had gathered. One of those women was Lydia, a Gentile God-worshipper from the city of Thyatira, a dealer in purple cloth. As she listened, the Lord enabled her to embrace Paul's message. Once she and her household were baptized, she urged, "Now that you have decided that I am a believer in the Lord, come and stay in my house." And she persuaded us.

Lydia's Conversion

SARAH FULLER

Lydia

Within the shell's center cave,
the place where she listens,
blushed, smooth, quiet—
purple lives.

Buried in this lone curl of home,
a river of indigo longing
and love's crimson heat,
an alchemy of reverent awe.
Just enough dye
for the hem of a robe
reached with empty hand.

Gathered at water's edge,
she invites more,
listens more,
her heart opens
even more
        to his Call,
till the whole cloth
is baptized into a lavish Yes.

—Julia Baker

FOR REFLECTION:

- Consider the role of color in this poem. We know that Lydia was a seller of purple cloth. What role does color have when reading a text or even praying?

- What images from your own life come to mind when you meditate on the final stanza of the poem?

- Consider writing a poem or prayer about any colors that come to mind.

PART 4

Resistance

RESISTING GENOCIDE: SHIPHRAH AND PUAH

READ: EXODUS 1:15–21

The king of Egypt spoke to two Hebrew midwives named Shiphrah and Puah: "When you are helping the Hebrew women give birth and you see the baby being born, if it's a boy, kill him. But if it's a girl, you can let her live." Now the two midwives respected God so they didn't obey the Egyptian king's order. Instead, they let the baby boys live.

So the king of Egypt called the two midwives and said to them, "Why are you doing this? Why are you letting the baby boys live?"

The two midwives said to Pharaoh, "Because Hebrew women aren't like Egyptian women. They're much stronger and give birth before any midwives can get to them." So God treated the midwives well, and the people kept on multiplying and became very strong. And because the midwives respected God, God gave them households of their own.

Resisting Genocide: Shiphrah and Puah DONA PARK

Shiphrah and Puah (Selah)

You drew me from the womb,
kept me safe at my mother's breast.
—Psalm 22:9 (author's translation)

Sudden summons are nothing new.
All their hours, appraised, are poised
between heaven and earth, like an eyebrow raised.

Moon, the shofar, moans, travails,
trailing clouds of iris, blood,
death's devouring, river's flood.

Passing through fields of swords upraised,
they gather valor
wisdom
faith
like scepters
They tell their truth. They disobey.

New moon, rejoice! No mourning today!
Learn them: Shif-rah. Pu-ah. Praise!
Let them again be household names!

Egyptian midwives, in midrash reading,
save the fathers, deliver a nation:
bouquet of babies, bright-eyed, breathing.

—Carmen Susana Horst

FOR REFLECTION:

- Note how the poem makes creative use of alliteration (e.g., "bouquet of babies, bright-eyed, breathing") and rhyme (e.g., reading/breathing, blood/flood, disobey/today). Read the poem aloud to fully appreciate the poet's use of sound.

- Ponder the image of Shiphrah and Puah. The poet invites us to praise these courageous examples of resistance and, evoking a more modern form of resilience and resistance, to say their names: "Shif-rah. Pu-ah."

- As you continue to look at the artwork, pay attention to the feelings it evokes. Offer a prayer for the midwives you know or for all those who assist in the intense process—full of pain, anticipation, and joy—of bringing new life into the world.

RAHAB HELPS THE SPIES ESCAPE

READ: JOSHUA 2:8–21

Before the spies bedded down, Rahab went up to them on the roof. She said to the men, "I know that the Lord has given you the land. Terror over you has overwhelmed us. The entire population of the land has melted down in fear because of you. We have heard how the Lord dried up the water of the Reed Sea in front of you when you left Egypt. We have also heard what you did to Sihon and Og, the two kings of the Amorites on the other side of the Jordan. You utterly wiped them out. We heard this and our hearts turned to water. Because of you, people can no longer work up their courage. This is because the Lord your God is God in heaven above and on earth below. Now, I have been loyal to you. So pledge to me by the Lord that you in turn will deal loyally with my family. Give me a sign of good faith. Spare the lives of my father, mother, brothers, and sisters, along with everything they own. Rescue us from death."

The men said to her, "We swear by our own lives to secure yours. If you don't reveal our mission, we will deal loyally and faithfully with you when the Lord gives us the land."

So she lowered the spies on a rope through the window. Her house was on the outer side of the city wall, and she lived inside the wall. Then she said to them, "Go toward the highlands so that those chasing you don't run into you. Hide there for three days until those chasing you return. Then you may go on your way."

The men said to her, "We won't be responsible for this pledge you made us swear unless, when we come into the land, you tie this red woven cord in the window through which you lowered us. Gather your father, your mother, your brothers, and your whole family into the house with you. Those who go outside the doors of your house into the street will have only themselves to blame for their own deaths. We won't be responsible. If anyone lays a hand on those who are with you in the house, we will take the blame for their death. But if you reveal our mission, we won't be responsible for this pledge you made us swear."

She said, "These things will happen just like you said." She sent them away and they went off. Then she tied the red cord in the window.

Rahab Helps the Spies Escape DONA PARK

Rehab, Joshua 2

Someone typed Rehab instead of Rahab, linking her story forever with a memory of my relative in a rehab care facility, victim to vertigo. For a time, his world spiraled in endless falling. His life, freedom, and dignity at stake, he was fully dependent on helpers, the almost invisible women who moved through his rooms.

* * *

Rahab decides who lives and who dies. She hides the spies under the flax, brings her mother, father, sisters, and brothers into her household for saving, betrays her neighbors. (Even their sheep and donkeys will not be spared.)

She keeps her own alive.

* * *

Invisible women scrubbing the floors, changing the bedsheets, holding the window open, caring for their own. Their eyes are the sheltering night or fields of flax in flower, their shoulders braced against indignities that scarlet their cheeks. They are more than the mothers of kings; the fates of nations hang from the ropes their fingers weave.

* * *

In fearful times, when your hearts are water, you lie helpless beneath the flax. You trust because you must.

Sometimes, you rise up and grasp the center of the great spiral.

—Kirsten Eve Beachy

FOR REFLECTION:

- This is a compressed lyric essay, using a typo as the premise for a poetic narrative. The lyric essay is an emerging, hybrid form that incorporates aspects of prose and poetry. It often takes the form of a personal essay and uses poetic devices to drive the narrative. A lyric essay experiments with language and ideas. An essay might record experiences, but a lyric essay creates them.

- The artwork depicts Rahab's rope as a kind of spiral. What might it mean for you to "rise up and grasp the center of the great spiral"?

- Experiment with writing your own lyric essay in response to these texts or the artwork.

DEBORAH: PROPHET AND JUDGE

READ: JUDGES 4:4–10

Now Deborah, a prophet, the wife of Lappidoth, was a leader of Israel at that time. She would sit under Deborah's palm tree between Ramah and Bethel in the Ephraim highlands, and the Israelites would come to her to settle disputes. She sent word to Barak, Abinoam's son, from Kedesh in Naphtali and said to him, "Hasn't the Lord, Israel's God, issued you a command? 'Go and assemble at Mount Tabor, taking ten thousand men from the people of Naphtali and Zebulun with you. I'll lure Sisera, the commander of Jabin's army, to assemble with his chariots and troops against you at the Kishon River, and then I'll help you overpower him.'"

Barak replied to her, "If you'll go with me, I'll go; but if not, I won't go."

Deborah answered, "I'll definitely go with you. However, the path you're taking won't bring honor to you, because the Lord will hand over Sisera to a woman." Then Deborah got up and went with Barak to Kedesh. He summoned Zebulun and Naphtali to Kedesh, and ten thousand men marched out behind him. Deborah marched out with him too.

Deborah: Prophet and Judge SARAH FULLER

Deborah: A Prayer on the Eve of Battle

O Lord, I am not a woman of war, but negotiation. Here I sit under the tree of justice you have given me, this palm between Ramah and Bethel, from where I may gaze at my very own patch of sky, stitched with stars or carried like a pale blue dress by doves or hawks, depending on what troubles the wind carries. From here I can look down into the valley and see the lamps of the village as they are lit, mothers calling their sons and daughters in for the evening meal. I am a mother to Israel, and my people call me the prophetess of stern softness. I am a mother to Israel and a wife to Lappidoth, even if it appears I must order a battlefield instead of a nursery. Future generations may call me fiery or drastic for taking actions most attributed to men. But you have put the fire in my belly, O Lord, and you have put the sword of prayer into my hands, your words planted in my heart like a thousand visions. Yes, I will call Barak, since not all negotiations can be dealt with under a tree. But first, I will sit a moment longer and think of the word honor, and how I wish it were not linked to bloodshed but brotherhood. What will a woman like me—my people's tightrope-walking prophetess-judge, their troubleshooter—do with the glory of gore and vindication?

—*Charity Gingerich*

FOR REFLECTION

- The scripture text describes Deborah not only as a prophet and judge but also as a woman and a war strategist. In this prayer/poem, the poet imagines Deborah struggling with the impending violence, the meaning of "honor," and the dubious "glory of gore and vindication." As you reflect on the image of Deborah seated beneath the palm tree, what else might be going through her mind?

- Who are the Deborah-like figures in your life?

- How does the Deborah in the poem feel about her role as a negotiator? Have you felt conflicted about an action you needed to take? Consider writing a prayer or poem about it.

ESTHER'S COURAGE AND CREATIVITY

READ: ESTHER 7:1–10

When the king and Haman came in for the banquet with Queen Esther, the king said to her, "This is the second day we've met for wine. What is your wish, Queen Esther? I'll give it to you. And what do you want? I'll do anything—even give you half the kingdom."

Queen Esther answered, "If I please the king, and if the king wishes, give me my life—that's my wish—and the lives of my people too. That's my desire. We have been sold—I and my people—to be wiped out, killed, and destroyed. If we simply had been sold as male and female slaves, I would have said nothing. But no enemy can compensate the king for this kind of damage."

King Ahasuerus said to Queen Esther, "Who is this person, and where is he? Who would dare do such a thing?"

Esther replied, "A man who hates, an enemy—this wicked Haman!" Haman was overcome with terror in the presence of the king and queen. Furious, the king got up and left the banquet for the palace garden. But Haman stood up to beg Queen Esther for his life. He saw clearly that the king's mood meant a bad end for him.

The king returned from the palace garden to the banquet room just as Haman was kneeling on the couch where Esther was reclining. "Will you even molest the queen while I am in the house?" the king said. The words had barely left the king's mouth before covering Haman's face with dread.

Harbona, one of the eunuchs serving the king, said, "Sir, look! There's the stake that Haman made for Mordecai, the man who spoke up and did something good for the king. It's standing at Haman's house—seventy-five feet high."

"Impale him on it!" the king ordered. So they impaled Haman on the very pole that he had set up for Mordecai, and the king's anger went away.

Esther's Courage and Creativity DONA PARK

Thinking about the Book of Esther, October 2023: A Senryu Sequence

Esther
good name
for a Mennonite aunt

her long curls
the golden cover
of my old children's Bible

to raise the scepter . . .
scent of
her oils and creams

white linen curtains and purple hangings
scorching wind
of the king's decree

sunbeam watching the MCC peace record spin

the scepter's shadow
pointing to
a new world

overkill
the legacy
of a 75-foot pole

poppy seed bagel how many civilians dead

—Daniel Shank Cruz

FOR REFLECTION:

- Senryu is a Japanese poetry form. Senryu poems are structurally similar to haiku in that they have three lines and often seventeen syllables. But whereas haiku generally focus on the natural world, senryu are usually about human nature and can take an ironic or darkly comedic tone. Short, compressed poetry is an invitation to consider and ponder a number of possible meanings.
- Esther's story can be read as a simple, straightforward heroic narrative of reversal, empowerment, and even revenge. As you contemplate the artwork, reflect on the poem, and reread the biblical account, what else do you see in this story?
- Experiment with writing a response or reflection using the senryu form.

AN UPSIDE-DOWN KINGDOM

READ: MATTHEW 5:3–12

> Happy are people who are hopeless, because the kingdom of heaven is theirs.
> Happy are people who grieve, because they will be made glad.
> Happy are people who are humble, because they will inherit the earth.
> Happy are people who are hungry and thirsty for righteousness, because they will be fed until they are full.
> Happy are people who show mercy, because they will receive mercy.
> Happy are people who have pure hearts, because they will see God.
> Happy are people who make peace, because they will be called God's children.
> Happy are people whose lives are harassed because they are righteous, because the kingdom of heaven is theirs.
> Happy are you when people insult you and harass you and speak all kinds of bad and false things about you, all because of me. Be full of joy and be glad, because you have a great reward in heaven. In the same way, people harassed the prophets who came before you.

An Upside-Down Kingdom DONA PARK

When?

Rapt they stand
on the slope
of the mount
intent on every word
from his mouth.

How can it be
in this time of tyranny
that we will see
the kingdom come,
that our inheritance
will be the earth,
that our children's stomachs
will be filled?

Maybe when the king is dead.
Surely there will never be
another Herod on the throne.

—Joseph Gascho

FOR REFLECTION:

- The poem ponders whether the kingdom can come while Herod is on the throne and concludes, "Surely there will never be / another Herod on the throne." Is the poet being ironic? Do you see other Herods today?

- It's hard to imagine how these words of Jesus must have sounded to the original audience. After reading the scripture passage and reflecting on the faces in the artwork, select one or two verses from the Beatitudes (Matthew 5:3–12) and write an inner monologue in the voice of one of the people depicted in the image.

- How might you react to these words of Jesus if he were speaking them today?

PART 5

Bondage and Liberation

LIBERATION FROM BONDAGE

READ: EXODUS 14:15–18, 21–31

Then the LORD said to Moses, "Why do you cry out to me? Tell the Israelites to get moving. As for you, lift your shepherd's rod, stretch out your hand over the sea, and split it in two so that the Israelites can go into the sea on dry ground. But me, I'll make the Egyptians stubborn so that they will go in after them, and I'll gain honor at the expense of Pharaoh, all his army, his chariots, and his cavalry. The Egyptians will know that I am the LORD, when I gain honor at the expense of Pharaoh, his chariots, and his cavalry." . . .

Then Moses stretched out his hand over the sea. The LORD pushed the sea back by a strong east wind all night, turning the sea into dry land. The waters were split into two. The Israelites walked into the sea on dry ground. The waters formed a wall for them on their right hand and on their left. The Egyptians chased them and went into the sea after them, all of Pharaoh's horses, chariots, and cavalry. As morning approached, the LORD looked down on the Egyptian camp from the column of lightning and cloud and threw the Egyptian camp into a panic. The LORD jammed their chariot wheels so that they wouldn't turn easily. The Egyptians said, "Let's get away from the Israelites, because the LORD is fighting for them against Egypt!"

Then the LORD said to Moses, "Stretch out your hand over the sea so that the water comes back and covers the Egyptians, their chariots, and their cavalry." So Moses stretched out his hand over the sea. At daybreak, the sea returned to its normal depth. The Egyptians were driving toward it, and the LORD tossed the Egyptians into the sea. The waters returned and covered the chariots and the cavalry, Pharaoh's entire army that had followed them into the sea. Not one of them remained. The Israelites, however, walked on dry ground through the sea. The waters formed a wall for them on their right hand and on their left.

The LORD rescued Israel from the Egyptians that day. Israel saw the Egyptians dead on the seashore. Israel saw the amazing power of the LORD against the Egyptians. The people were in awe of the LORD, and they believed in the LORD and in his servant Moses.

Liberation from Bondage MATTHEW REGIER

Some Naïve Questions (Exodus 14 and 15)

1. If the Israelites were already out of town, why would God bother to harden Pharaoh's heart?
2. Describe the precise sort of glory that results from a vastly superior being manipulating the natural world to slaughter an entire army, complete with chariots and horses.
3. Just how culpable were the horses?
4. Might drowning a smaller number of men and/or horses have sufficed to convince the Egyptians that the Lord is mighty in battle?
5. Did Pharaoh drown along with his army, and if so, was his successor established after the waters swept over him?
6. On which shore were the dead deposited, or were some on either side?
7. If not one member of the army survived, how long did it take for the Egyptians to discover them?
8. How accurate was the expectation that once the Egyptian soldiers (and horses) were washed up with their lungs full of the Red Sea, the mothers and fathers and wives and children left behind would worship and fear the God of Israel?
9. Would a discussion of "worship" and "fear" as related but not identical terms be useful here?
10. In light of all these events, how exactly would you define "unfailing love"?
11. Which of the participants in this narrative might seem most sympathetic to contemporary audiences, depending on their particular contexts?
12. How might this narrative be read by (a) the spiritual descendants of those who fled Pharaoh's army; (b) citizens of the planet's most powerful nation, supplier of massive weaponry to the spiritual descendants of those who fled Pharaoh's army; (c) the inhabitants of an impoverished, walled enclave now largely destroyed by the spiritual descendants of those who fled Pharaoh's army?
13. Which category most closely describes you?
14. Are these appropriate questions? Why or why not?
15. Having contemplated this narrative and the songs of Moses and Miriam, do you find yourself (a) desiring to sing praises to the Lord, who is highly exalted; (b) terrified; (c) seized by a mysterious trembling; (d) something else? Please explain.

—*Jeff Gundy*

FOR REFLECTION:

- This is a list poem in the form of questions, which take on the form of a text or exam. In such poems, the lists often build on each other and help to drive the poem.
- After reflecting on the scripture passage and the artwork, choose one or two questions from the poem at random and use the space below to gather your thoughts for a response.
- How does the exam question format affect how you read this scripture passage?

HEALING ON THE SABBATH

READ: LUKE 6:1–11

One Sabbath, as Jesus was going through the wheat fields, his disciples were picking the heads of wheat, rubbing them in their hands, and eating them. Some Pharisees said, "Why are you breaking the Sabbath law?"

Jesus replied, "Haven't you read what David and his companions did when they were hungry? He broke the Law by going into God's house and eating the bread of the presence, which only the priests can eat. He also gave some of the bread to his companions." Then he said to them, "The Human One is Lord of the Sabbath."

On another Sabbath, Jesus entered a synagogue to teach. A man was there whose right hand was withered. The legal experts and the Pharisees were watching him closely to see if he would heal on the Sabbath. They were looking for a reason to bring charges against him. Jesus knew their thoughts, so he said to the man with the withered hand, "Get up and stand in front of everyone." He got up and stood there. Jesus said to the legal experts and Pharisees, "Here's a question for you: Is it legal on the Sabbath to do good or to do evil, to save life or to destroy it?" Looking around at them all, he said to the man, "Stretch out your hand." So he did and his hand was made healthy. They were furious and began talking with each other about what to do to Jesus.

Healing on the Sabbath

RANDY HORST

Another Sabbath

Another Sabbath, a double rest, the holy high days
that Elohim hates for how they've withered us
and turned our compassion to piety, our pity
to sufficiency, our imagination for justice to
an imagination for burdens. How we have kept ourselves
on our holy days, separate from everything,
including him.

How we have bound our clinging scrolls, our rolls of expectation,
precedent perfected on unbroken generations.
How we have elaborated our laws, and elevated
the labyrinth of our contracts, above our own instincts
for compassion. How we have modeled into our minds,
above us in the crownworks of our enclosure, caricatures
of Zion, considering everything
but compassion.

Another Sabbath, another rest. But rest is no rest,
for the half of him who has had no rest from resting.
And synagogue is no shelter for pariahs, the partially broken,
the heavy ones, upon whom deprecations have come
to settle. For we have forgotten our chief joy.
Forgotten the glory, and preferred the certainty of our scripts
to the vulnerability of our brethren. Our morals are strong
but muscle-bound, the tendons have seized upon each other
and we cannot act. For the center below the center
is withered.

Watch him. The one too clear to see, too good to trust,
too simple to understand. Be careful; he may unmend you.
I am bitter, I am full, I am half asleep, and it seems he would gather me
into I know not what, and I am afraid with whom. The son of man,
this mother hen, this healer, the one
for whom caesuras made caesura:
He says stretch out your hand.

—Obi Martin

FOR REFLECTION:

- What has been your experience of the larger question raised by the poem? Were you raised in a church that was seemingly bound by tradition or allowed rules to take precedence over compassion?

- Although not many mainstream churches in the United States today attempt to restrict what members can do on the Sabbath, some states still enforce so-called blue laws, legally restricting the sale of certain products on Sundays. Do the rhythms of your day change at all on Sunday? How have you experienced Sabbath rest? How have you experienced Sabbath freedom?

- When have you experienced Christ asking you to stretch forth your hand for healing?

JESUS' ARREST IN THE GARDEN OF GETHSEMANE

READ: JOHN 18:1–12

After he said these things, Jesus went out with his disciples and crossed over to the other side of the Kidron Valley. He and his disciples entered a garden there. Judas, his betrayer, also knew the place because Jesus often gathered there with his disciples. Judas brought a company of soldiers and some guards from the chief priests and Pharisees. They came there carrying lanterns, torches, and weapons. Jesus knew everything that was to happen to him, so he went out and asked, "Who are you looking for?"

They answered, "Jesus the Nazarene."

He said to them, "I Am." (Judas, his betrayer, was standing with them.) When he said, "I Am," they shrank back and fell to the ground. He asked them again, "Who are you looking for?"

They said, "Jesus the Nazarene."

Jesus answered, "I told you, 'I Am.' If you are looking for me, then let these people go." This was so that the word he had spoken might be fulfilled: "I didn't lose anyone of those whom you gave me."

Then Simon Peter, who had a sword, drew it and struck the high priest's servant, cutting off his right ear. (The servant's name was Malchus.) Jesus told Peter, "Put your sword away! Am I not to drink the cup the Father has given me?" Then the company of soldiers, the commander, and the guards from the Jewish leaders took Jesus into custody.

Jesus' Arrest in the Garden of Gethsemane RANDY HORST

Until Peace Comes

On the hillside wild *anemone coronaria* burgeon
above the lake where those with ears
hungry for bread and fish would gather
to listen. To the people he said,

love your enemies, be merciful,

be like the lilies of the field,
sustained by trust and by goodness to one another.
Children ran to him as to a loving father

and he blessed them.

In the garden he stooped to pick up the white petal,
severed ear, leaned in to touch the face
of Malchus, auricle, a red and sudden bloom,

hand outstretched to stop the flow of blood.

A sword in a fisherman's fist; a fishing knife
to mend nets, to clean, scale, fillet tilapia, wielded
by a hand closed into a fist; a fist. Vengeance
begets generations without ears,

he warned those who lived by the sword.

At the touch of his hand, the ear-flap like a fin, pinna,
was sealed in place, healed,
but what became of Malchus, his face-
to-face encounter?

Will the heart open, or remain heart-deaf?
How long must love suffer?
Inscribed with a blade

on the cross, the acrostic forming the name,

the one who insists on love, pierced
palms, dorsa, *anemone coronaria* blooming.

—*Connie T. Braun*

FOR REFLECTION:

- The scripture passage compresses a great deal of meaning into a brief dramatic encounter between Jesus, Judas, Simon Peter, and a servant named Malchus. As armed guards prepare to arrest Jesus, Peter lashes out in fear and anger, prompting a rebuke from Jesus. Although the story is related in all three of the synoptic gospels, only in Luke's account of the story does Jesus heal Malchus (Luke 22:51).

- Take some time to reflect on the images in the artwork. What do you know about the *anemone coronaria*, or poppy anemone? Is the blade a fisherman's knife or a dangerous weapon?

- "How long," the poet asks, "must love suffer?" What does this mean to you?

- What did Jesus mean when he said, "Let the person who has ears, hear" (Matthew 11:15)?

PILATE WASHES HIS HANDS

READ: MATTHEW 27:15–24

It was customary during the festival for the governor to release to the crowd one prisoner, whomever they might choose. At that time there was a well-known prisoner named Jesus Barabbas. When the crowd had come together, Pilate asked them, "Whom would you like me to release to you, Jesus Barabbas or Jesus who is called Christ?" He knew that the leaders of the people had handed him over because of jealousy.

While he was serving as judge, his wife sent this message to him, "Leave that righteous man alone. I've suffered much today in a dream because of him."

But the chief priests and the elders persuaded the crowds to ask for Barabbas and kill Jesus. The governor said, "Which of the two do you want me to release to you?"

"Barabbas," they replied.

Pilate said, "Then what should I do with Jesus who is called Christ?"

They all said, "Crucify him!"

But he said, "Why? What wrong has he done?"

They shouted even louder, "Crucify him!"

Pilate saw that he was getting nowhere and that a riot was starting. So he took water and washed his hands in front of the crowd. "I'm innocent of this man's blood," he said. "It's your problem."

Pilate Washes His Hands MATTHEW REGIER

Then Pilate

In her dream my wife
saw it all:
Barabbas, Jesus sweating

blood and light, the cross.
(How much of
the cross is the road to the cross?)

"He's innocent," she said.
"I've suffered.
You can't imagine. All day.

Don't touch him." So I didn't.
Or I did.
I was innocent, I told them. No.

How much of justice
is looking
the other way?
How much of innocence
is the way
the wind blows?
When I washed my hands
they were too
big for the water.

—*Keith Ratzlaff*

FOR REFLECTION:

- Often overlooked in the crucifixion narrative, the details of Pilate's wife and Pilate's own effort to distance himself from the judgment against Jesus add poignancy to this familiar story.

- With whom do you identify most in this passage? Was Pilate following the counsel of his wife? Or did she intend for Pilate to intervene on behalf of Jesus?

- In the space below, reflect on a time when you tried to wash your hands of moral responsibility.

CHRIST'S DEATH AND THE NEW COVENANT

READ: HEBREWS 9:11–14

But Christ has appeared as the high priest of the good things that have happened. He passed through the greater and more perfect meeting tent, which isn't made by human hands (that is, it's not a part of this world). He entered the holy of holies once for all by his own blood, not by the blood of goats or calves, securing our deliverance for all time. If the blood of goats and bulls and the sprinkled ashes of cows made spiritually contaminated people holy and clean, how much more will the blood of Jesus wash our consciences clean from dead works in order to serve the living God? He offered himself to God through the eternal Spirit as a sacrifice without any flaw.

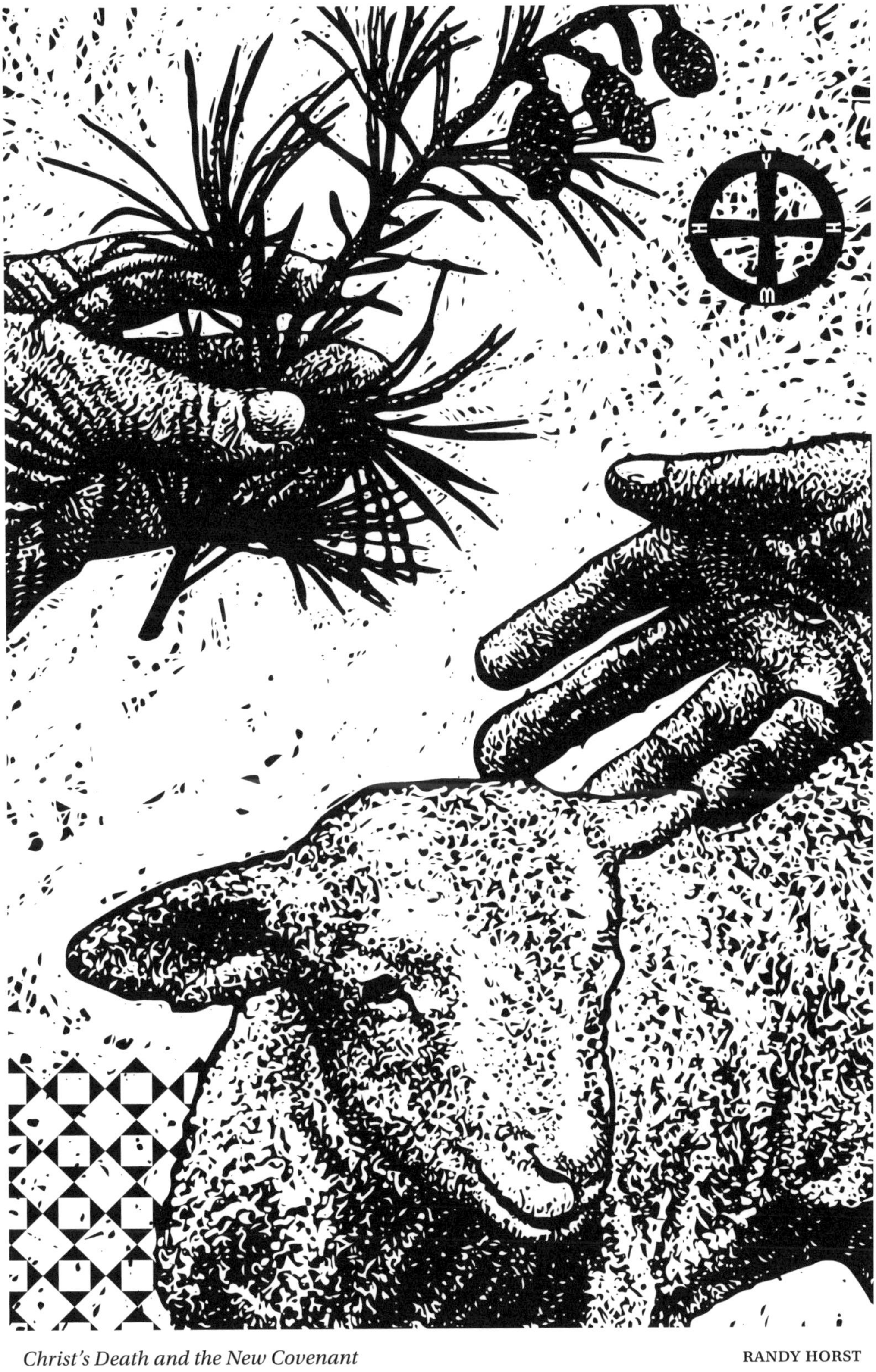

Christ's Death and the New Covenant RANDY HORST

Except One

Everyone dies leaving something undone.
The farmer, a field not harvested, the heavy
grains bending the stalks. A teacher gone,
but her student with one more question. The
pastor, a sermon written, but not preached,
the shepherd with his sheep not sheared,
as summer arrives. The old cedar toppled,
its seeds spilled on thin soil. Everything
dies, leaving something undone.

Why are the flags always at half-mast? So
much death to remember, and then to try to
forget. Everyone dies with work undone.
Others grip the dropped tools, and continue
sowing, teaching, healing. Seasons, lives,
and promises are renewed. The same, yet
different. The work doesn't end. A new
cedar grows and grows. But we die soon,
leaving something undone.

—Leonard Nolt

FOR REFLECTION:

- The book of Hebrews focuses on the human suffering of Jesus in the context of the rituals of sacrifice from the Old Testament. But it also depicts Jesus as the great high priest who is the mediator between humanity and God, and whose suffering has brought an end to these traditions of sacrifice.

- The artwork hints at these themes while also referencing another Old Testament text (Ezekiel 17:22–24) in which God takes a sprig from the mighty cedar tree—a sturdy and beautiful wood often used in the Old Testament for the construction of important buildings—and replants it to represent a new covenant. In New Testament interpretation, this sprig will become a full tree, reaching its full height, in the Messiah, in Jesus, the Christ.

- What work, as the poet suggests, is left undone in the world? What work is left undone in your life?

PART 6

Women and Mothering

RUTH AND NAOMI

READ: RUTH 1:8–22

Naomi said to her daughters-in-law, "Go, turn back, each of you to the household of your mother. May the LORD deal faithfully with you, just as you have done with the dead and with me. May the LORD provide for you so that you may find security, each woman in the household of her husband." Then she kissed them, and they lifted up their voices and wept.

But they replied to her, "No, instead we will return with you, to your people."

Naomi replied, "Turn back, my daughters. Why would you go with me? Will there again be sons in my womb, that they would be husbands for you? Turn back, my daughters. Go. I am too old for a husband. If I were to say that I have hope, even if I had a husband tonight, and even more, if I were to bear sons—would you wait until they grew up? Would you refrain from having a husband? No, my daughters. This is more bitter for me than for you, since the LORD's will has come out against me."

Then they lifted up their voices and wept again. Orpah kissed her mother-in-law, but Ruth stayed with her. Naomi said, "Look, your sister-in-law is returning to her people and to her gods. Turn back after your sister-in-law."

But Ruth replied, "Don't urge me to abandon you, to turn back from following after you. Wherever you go, I will go; and wherever you stay, I will stay. Your people will be my people, and your God will be my God. Wherever you die, I will die, and there I will be buried. May the LORD do this to me and more so if even death separates me from you." When Naomi saw that Ruth was determined to go with her, she stopped speaking to her about it.

So both of them went along until they arrived at Bethlehem. When they arrived at Bethlehem, the whole town was excited on account of them, and the women of the town asked, "Can this be Naomi?"

She replied to them, "Don't call me Naomi, but call me Mara, for the Almighty has made me very bitter. I went away full, but the LORD has returned me empty. Why would you call me Naomi, when the LORD has testified against me, and the Almighty has deemed me guilty?"

Thus Naomi returned. And Ruth the Moabite, her daughter-in-law, returned with her from the territory of Moab. They arrived in Bethlehem at the beginning of the barley harvest.

Ruth and Naomi LISA OBIREK

Ruth

Like a seed, she drifts,
widowed, a Moabite,
into the land of Naomi,
into the arms of a field.

Like a seed, she waits
as she gleans the fallen
grain, bending toward
our fertile earth,

and is seen, then chosen
to carry the Seed of Promise,
of Hope for our waiting,
hungry world.

—Jean Janzen

FOR REFLECTION:

- The story of Ruth and Naomi describes a friendship—a bond of trust and loyalty more deeply rooted than other claims on identity or allegiance. The risk that Ruth takes creates a space for transformation. What is the seed of transformation that is waiting to take root in you?

- The white space in the artwork seems to be pointing Ruth and Naomi to an unknown future. As you reflect on the image, what does the white space elicit in you?

- Where else does your eye linger in the image? Why?

GOD'S PRESENCE

READ: PSALM 139:7–18

Where could I go to get away from your spirit?
    Where could I go to escape your presence?
If I went up to heaven, you would be there.
    If I went down to the grave, you would be there too!
If I could fly on the wings of dawn,
    stopping to rest only on the far side of the ocean—
        even there your hand would guide me;
        even there your strong hand would hold me tight!
If I said, "The darkness will definitely hide me;
    the light will become night around me,"
    even then the darkness isn't too dark for you!
        Nighttime would shine bright as day,
        because darkness is the same as light to you!

You are the one who created my innermost parts;
    you knit me together while I was still in my mother's womb.
I give thanks to you that I was marvelously set apart.
    Your works are wonderful—I know that very well.
My bones weren't hidden from you
    when I was being put together in a secret place,
    when I was being woven together in the deep parts of the earth.
Your eyes saw my embryo,
    and on your scroll every day was written that was being formed for me,
    before any one of them had yet happened.
God, your plans are incomprehensible to me!
    Their total number is countless!
If I tried to count them—they outnumber grains of sand!
    If I came to the very end—I'd still be with you.

God's Presence RANDY HORST

Divine Parent

You gave me life
close to a mothering heart
on this earthly plain
until she could hold me
in her calloused hands.
From the beginning
she loved me with love
she knew from you.

She introduced me
to you, Heavenly Father,
though you know me
better than I know myself.
Mother pointed the way
to Jesus and your kingdom
here on Planet Earth and in
the wider Universe of Light.

Like a bird soaring in the sky
your Spirit keeps an eye
on children everywhere
while with heart and mind
we pray for freedom from fear,
for a heart and world at peace.
Love guides grace-filled hands
to help justice increase.

Mother taught me
to pray and give thanks
for the love and provision
that is mine to share.
She had a stake in faith
that helped her through
clouds and fire. This way
of Jesus now leads me
to you, Mothering God.

—*Ruth Naylor*

FOR REFLECTION:

- Spend some time gazing at the image and reflecting on the scripture text and the poem.

- Have you ever experienced anxiety or profound loneliness? If so, this psalm offers words of great comfort and assurance. Why is it sometimes so hard to claim these promises?

- The poem identifies a key person who embodied the qualities of unconditional love described by the psalmist. Who is that person (or persons) for you? What specific moments do you recall that made that love real for you? Write a poem or prayer about these moments.

WOMAN WISDOM

READ: PROVERBS 8:1–12

Doesn't Wisdom cry out
    and Understanding shout?
Atop the heights along the path,
    at the crossroads she takes her stand.
By the gate before the city,
    at the entrances she shouts:

I cry out to you, people;
    my voice goes out to all of humanity.
Understand skill, you who are naive.
    Take this to heart, you fools.
Listen, for I speak things that are correct;
    from my lips comes what is right.
My mouth utters the truth;
    my lips despise wickedness.
All the words of my mouth are righteous;
    nothing in them is twisted or crooked.
All of them are straightforward to those who understand,
    and upright for the knowledgeable.
Take my instruction rather than silver,
    knowledge rather than choice gold.
Wisdom is better than pearls;
    nothing is more delightful than she.

I, Wisdom, dwell with prudence;
    I have found knowledge and discretion.

Woman Wisdom

DONA PARK

Listen

When in one season the world's too warm and then too cold, wind bellowing as if to make the point, even the trusty kale stiff in its bed.

When the woman you love most stopped breathing on this day one month ago.

When the phone call.

When murder is incessant, unseen and far away.

When the stillness in her hands came true, when all this, is there a voice, does Wisdom speak?

* * *

Comfort one morning waking in the dark, as if her sensibility had flourished while you slept:

I've been up before the stars praying
for you and your children, praying justice
and kindness, listening to the speech of tiger
and hare, elephant and dove,
to the rustle of date palms and the small sea
turtle shuffling down the beach, to the birches
each summer burning, I whisper
from their ashes in fireweed and ferns
unfurling, I'm here at the height
of land, beside the way, at the crossroads
I take your hand.

I'm always arriving in that moment
before your anger flares, breathe in, breathe
out, breath given *before*
the mountains had been shaped,
before the hills, I was brought forth,
before the sea was crashing, I helped to hammer the keys
of the mbira, instrument plinking a story
by the thumbs of one who knows,
I delight in each person I circle
within my arms, we make soup,

rice, we eat laughing although we have
no common words, we travel
with the humble ox through the night, alert
for that rare tune
through an open window,
doorway, at the height
of land, *beside the way, at the cross*
roads we take a stand
and listen.

—Barbara Nickel

FOR REFLECTION:

- "Is there a voice," the poet asks, "does Wisdom speak?" As you reflect on the scripture passage, gaze on the image, and ponder the poem, how do you answer this question?

- How does the voice of Wisdom speak to you?

- How does the voice of Wisdom speak through you?

- If you were to sketch Woman Wisdom, as personified in Proverbs, what would she look like?

THE WOMAN AT THE WELL

READ: JOHN 4:4–18, 25–29

Jesus had to go through Samaria. He came to a Samaritan city called Sychar, which was near the land Jacob had given to his son Joseph. Jacob's well was there. Jesus was tired from his journey, so he sat down at the well. It was about noon.

A Samaritan woman came to the well to draw water. Jesus said to her, "Give me some water to drink." His disciples had gone into the city to buy him some food.

The Samaritan woman asked, "Why do you, a Jewish man, ask for something to drink from me, a Samaritan woman?" (Jews and Samaritans didn't associate with each other.)

Jesus responded, "If you recognized God's gift and who is saying to you, 'Give me some water to drink,' you would be asking him and he would give you living water."

The woman said to him, "Sir, you don't have a bucket and the well is deep. Where would you get this living water? You aren't greater than our father Jacob, are you? He gave this well to us, and he drank from it himself, as did his sons and his livestock."

Jesus answered, "Everyone who drinks this water will be thirsty again, but whoever drinks from the water that I will give will never be thirsty again. The water that I give will become in those who drink it a spring of water that bubbles up into eternal life."

The woman said to him, "Sir, give me this water, so that I will never be thirsty and will never need to come here to draw water!"

Jesus said to her, "Go, get your husband, and come back here."

The woman replied, "I don't have a husband."

"You are right to say, 'I don't have a husband,'" Jesus answered. "You've had five husbands, and the man you are with now isn't your husband. You've spoken the truth."...

The woman said, "I know that the Messiah is coming, the one who is called the Christ. When he comes, he will teach everything to us."

Jesus said to her, "I Am—the one who speaks with you."

Just then, Jesus' disciples arrived and were shocked that he was talking with a woman. But no one asked, "What do you want?" or "Why are you talking with her?" The woman put down her water jar and went into the city. She said to the people, "Come and see a man who has told me everything I've done! Could this man be the Christ?"

The Woman at the Well RANDY HORST

The Woman at the Well Speaks

I had a reputation. But not what you think.
Even as a child of Sychar, I was known
for my questions. "Why don't boys
carry the water jars?" "Why can't
a girl memorize the Torah?" These
my mother tried to shoo away
like sparrows in the rafters, till eventually
I asked what her broom couldn't reach
(or maybe she needed the answer too),
so she sent me to the village priest.
"Why is the word for god, ba'al,
the word we use for husband? Isn't that
blasphemy?" I asked him on the street.
He pretended not to hear, but somehow
word got round. When the matchmaker
sat down for lunch with news of a widower
old as Methuselah, I left to fetch water
and met a Jewish stranger at Jacob's Well.
"Will you give me a drink?" he said, lifting
the silence between us like Jacob heaving
the cistern stone when he met Rachel.
When I asked for the gift of living water,
Jesus said, "Go, call your ba'al,
and come back." "I have no ba'al," I said,
then caught his wordplay when he smiled.
If you want to believe I had five husbands,
go ahead, but you'll miss the intricacy
of our dance. Five ba'al? Gods
of five Assyrian cities allegedly defiling
Samaritan blood. And the ba'al we live
with now? Imperial Rome, same
as the Jews. "I Am," Jesus told me,
words Yahweh spoke to Moses
from the burning bush. That's when
illumination struck. I recognized my ba'al.
My one and only. Rachel left her sheep
as she ran with her news. I left my water jar.

—*Shari Miller Wagner*

FOR REFLECTION:

- This poem provides a commentary on the scripture passage that opens up new perspectives on this story of Jesus' encounter with the woman at the well. Reread the scripture passage through the lens of the poem. How does your perspective change? Take several minutes to gaze at the image. Do you see anything that you hadn't seen before?

- Have you had an encounter with the divine that changed you? The woman in the scripture text leaves her water jar. What have you left behind? Reflect in the space below.

ABIGAIL BRINGS A GIFT TO DAVID

READ: 1 SAMUEL 25:14–19, 23–28, 32–35

One of Nabal's servants told his wife Abigail, "David sent messengers from the wilderness to greet our master, but he just yelled at them. But the men were very good to us and didn't mistreat us. Nothing of ours went missing the whole time we were out with them in the fields. In fact, the whole time we were with them, watching our sheep, they were a protective wall around us both night and day. Think about that and see what you can do, because trouble is coming for our master and his whole household. But he's such a despicable person no one can speak to him."

Abigail quickly took two hundred loaves of bread, two skins of wine, five sheep ready for cooking, five seahs of roasted grain, one hundred raisin cakes, and two hundred fig cakes. She loaded all this on donkeys and told her servants, "Go on ahead of me. I'll be right behind you." But she didn't tell her husband Nabal. . . .

When Abigail saw David, she quickly got off her donkey and fell facedown before him, bowing low to the ground. She fell at his feet and said, "Put the blame on me, my master! But please let me, your servant, speak to you directly. Please listen to what your servant has to say. Please, my master, pay no attention to this despicable man Nabal. He's exactly what his name says he is! His name means fool, and he is foolish! But I myself, your servant, didn't see the young men that you, my master, sent. I pledge, my master, as surely as the LORD lives and as you live, that the LORD has held you back from bloodshed and taking vengeance into your own hands! But now let your enemies and those who seek to harm my master be exactly like Nabal! Here is a gift, which your servant has brought to my master. Please let it be given to the young men who follow you, my master. Please forgive any offense by your servant. . . .

David said to Abigail, "Bless the LORD God of Israel, who sent you to meet me today! And bless you and your good judgment for preventing me from shedding blood and taking vengeance into my own hands today! Otherwise, as surely as the LORD God of Israel lives—the one who kept me from hurting you—if you hadn't come quickly and met up with me, there wouldn't be one single one who urinates on a wall left come morning." Then David accepted everything she had brought for him. "Return home in peace," he told her. "Be assured that I've heard your request and have agreed to it."

Abigail Brings a Gift to David — DONA PARK

The Tale of Abigail

A man called Nabal was very rich
and he was harsh and evil in his dealings
and Abigail his wife was intelligent and beautiful.

One day, not-yet-king David sent peace to Nabal and requested food
and Nabal said, "Who is David? I cannot keep track of so many servants."
So David sent four hundred of his men with strapped swords.

Now Abigail heard of the army coming against her evil husband.
Then she took two jugs of wine and two hundred loaves of bread
and five sheep and five measures of roasted grain
and a hundred cakes of raisins and two hundred cakes of figs
and loaded the offering onto donkeys.
She told David, "My lord, accept my gift from your servant and
forgive the offense of your servant."

And David blessed the Lord God of Israel.
And David blessed her.

Then Nabal's heart died within him
so that he became like a stone when he heard.
Then Nabal died.

Then David sent a proposal to Abigail.

ABIGAIL, A PRIESTESS OF PEACE

The way of ancient storytellers spares readers of most judgments. Instead, their connecting words bridge events. They move the story forward while leaving interpretations open to the listeners.

Interpretations of this story abound. Perhaps medieval priests interpreted this story as a fairy tale, dark and satisfying and just. Abigail was rewarded for her sense of honor with more honor—a kingly marriage proposal. Today, many of us have heard a story about a demure woman and the attractiveness of meekness. Maybe it was Abigail's humility that prompted David's proposal.

Like Mary after her, Abigail interceded on the behalf of others. She went between Nabal and David, two men bent on bringing shame and violence upon one another. She was a priestess of peace. She presented generous harvests of food as her priestly offering.

Abigail may have felt various judgments on her. She married David and, according to the Greek translation of the Hebrew scriptures, named their firstborn son Daniel, or "God is my judge."

—Carita Keim

FOR REFLECTION

- The poem condenses the story of Abigail. Start your reflection by reading the entire chapter (1 Samuel 25). Reflect again on the image. What lingers with you about Abigail—her character or her actions as a diplomatic emissary between David and Nabal?

- This poem repeats words such as *and, then,* and *so*. How does repetition help you engage the poem?

- The poet offers some reflections at the end of the poem. Abigail may have felt judgments on her. When have you felt the judgments of others? How did you respond?

- Abigail interceded for others with offerings of food. Can you think of times when you have had to intercede? When have you been a diplomat or a peacemaker?

PART 7

The Body of Christ

BAPTISM OF JESUS

READ: MATTHEW 3:13–17

At that time Jesus came from Galilee to the Jordan River so that John would baptize him. John tried to stop him and said, "I need to be baptized by you, yet you come to me?"

Jesus answered, "Allow me to be baptized now. This is necessary to fulfill all righteousness."

So John agreed to baptize Jesus. When Jesus was baptized, he immediately came up out of the water. Heaven was opened to him, and he saw the Spirit of God coming down like a dove and resting on him. A voice from heaven said, "This is my Son whom I dearly love; I find happiness in him."

Baptism of Jesus MATTHEW REGIER

sons of water

water into water
like rain on the jordan
two sons from the waters
of elizabeth and mary the
waters of their wombs and
the trees they saw all blood
and branch the sound of heart
and the sound of earth outside
and in the child from nowhere
becoming flesh like words
and the man becoming spirit
becoming matter and over
and over water becoming
water until the river
dries up

—Patrick Friesen

FOR REFLECTION:

- In this poem, Patrick Friesen reflects on the "Word made flesh"— the deep mysteries of the incarnation and the sacrament of baptism. In the end, matter and spirit are as indistinguishable as "rain on the jordan / . . . water becoming / water."

- How do spirit and matter converge for you? What words or images have helped you express this reality?

- One could see this as a "shape poem," a form of concrete poetry in which the words take on a shape related to the subject matter, here possibly a drop of water or even the belly of a pregnant woman. As you reflect on the texts and image, consider responding with a shape poem or a sketch.

MARY MAGDALENE WITNESSES THE RESURRECTED JESUS

READ: JOHN 20:11–18

Mary stood outside near the tomb, crying. As she cried, she bent down to look into the tomb. She saw two angels dressed in white, seated where the body of Jesus had been, one at the head and one at the foot. The angels asked her, "Woman, why are you crying?"

She replied, "They have taken away my Lord, and I don't know where they've put him." As soon as she had said this, she turned around and saw Jesus standing there, but she didn't know it was Jesus.

Jesus said to her, "Woman, why are you crying? Who are you looking for?"

Thinking he was the gardener, she replied, "Sir, if you have carried him away, tell me where you have put him and I will get him."

Jesus said to her, "Mary."

She turned and said to him in Aramaic, "Rabbouni" (which means *Teacher*).

Jesus said to her, "Don't hold on to me, for I haven't yet gone up to my Father. Go to my brothers and sisters and tell them, 'I'm going up to my Father and your Father, to my God and your God.'"

Mary Magdalene left and announced to the disciples, "I've seen the Lord." Then she told them what he said to her.

Mary Magdalene Witnesses the Resurrected Jesus MATTHEW REGIER

Meditation on John 20:1–18

In the beginning, on the first day, Jesus, rising, apparently took the time
to roll the cloth covering his head and place it, neatly, to the side.

Before astonishment and disbelief, before breaking bread on the beach,
before the disciples spread and said, "I have seen the Lord,"
before house churches and persecutions, before co-optation and Constantine
and the entire tired history of crusades and inquisitions and witch hunts,
before enslaving and stealing land in the name of this Jewish man,
long before all this, he made his bed, as his mother had undoubtedly taught him.

I think of a line from a poem by Adrienne Rich.
Moved by grief at what has been destroyed,
the poet resolves to cast her lot with
"those who age after age, perversely,
with no extraordinary power, reconstitute the world."[1]

I think of those who plant the seeds in fields ravaged by war,
who mend the garments made ragged by violence, who bake the bread,
mind the children, make the fire while the men are gone,
conscripted into someone's grand plan to save the world by conquering it.
I think of those who bathe the body, anoint it with myrrh and aloes,
who watch and weep.

You have to bend down to enter the tomb, to even look within it.
You must lower yourself to the ground.
For centuries, the co-opted church has wanted to ascend, to build spires and
endowments, to raise money and armies, to be the one triumphal truth.

From the beginning, it was clear: Unless you get low,
you will not enter the place of new life.
Unless you weep over what has been destroyed, you will not see His risen form.
The work of Resurrection begins by tending to what matters—bodies, beds, bread.
From this lowly place, we rise with Him, to refashion the world until
all bodies are minded, fed, loved, wept over, restored, reconstituted.

—*Sheri Hostetler*

1 From "Natural Resources," in *The Dream of a Common Language: Poems 1974–1977* (W. W. Norton, 1978), 67.

FOR REFLECTION:

- The artwork accompanying the scripture passage depicts Mary Magdalene's encounter with the "gardener" at the empty tomb. But at first glance it could also evoke associations with Adam and Eve in the garden of Eden. As you linger on the image, what connections come to mind between these two crucial moments in the biblical story?

- The poem begins by calling our attention to the cloth that covered Jesus' face, "folded up in its own place" (John 20:7). Why do you think this detail is important?

- Take some time to reflect on this line from the poem: "The work of Resurrection begins by tending to what matters—bodies, beds, bread." What rises in you?

PHILIP AND THE ETHIOPIAN EUNUCH

READ: ACTS 8:26–40

An angel from the Lord spoke to Philip, "At noon, take the road that leads from Jerusalem to Gaza." (This is a desert road.) So he did. Meanwhile, an Ethiopian man was on his way home from Jerusalem, where he had come to worship. He was a eunuch and an official responsible for the entire treasury of Candace. (Candace is the title given to the Ethiopian queen.) He was reading the prophet Isaiah while sitting in his carriage. The Spirit told Philip, "Approach this carriage and stay with it."

Running up to the carriage, Philip heard the man reading the prophet Isaiah. He asked, "Do you really understand what you are reading?"

The man replied, "Without someone to guide me, how could I?" Then he invited Philip to climb up and sit with him. This was the passage of scripture he was reading:

Like a sheep he was led to the slaughter
    and like a lamb before its shearer is silent
    so he didn't open his mouth.
In his humiliation justice was taken away from him.
    Who can tell the story of his descendants
        because his life was taken from the earth?

The eunuch asked Philip, "Tell me, about whom does the prophet say this? Is he talking about himself or someone else?" Starting with that passage, Philip proclaimed the good news about Jesus to him. As they went down the road, they came to some water.

The eunuch said, "Look! Water! What would keep me from being baptized?" He ordered that the carriage halt. Both Philip and the eunuch went down to the water, where Philip baptized him. When they came up out of the water, the Lord's Spirit suddenly took Philip away. The eunuch never saw him again but went on his way rejoicing. Philip found himself in Azotus. He traveled through that area, preaching the good news in all the cities until he reached Caesarea.

Philip and the Ethiopian Eunuch MATTHEW REGIER

What chains have I been asked to wear

Inspired by the life and example of Margaret Hellwart of Beutelsbach (b. 1568), an Anabaptist who was chained in her kitchen in an attempt to keep her from teaching about Jesus and converting others, and by the question the Ethiopian eunuch asks of Philip: "Look, here is water! What is to prevent me from being baptized?"

(lyrics set to the tune "My Shepherd Will Supply My Need")

What chains have I been asked to wear that make my footsteps small,
made not of Spirit's breath but in the shape of human law?
And do I wear them willingly, though they trip me and I fall?
O teach my steps what freedom means, Great Love who frees us all.

What chains do I expect another child of God to wear?
What has my living helped to forge, what cage, what pain to bear?
What door would need to open wide for me to see you there?
O Spirit, show me how to grieve, to cup this needed prayer.

What chains today do I still choose for body or for soul,
and what will be the consequence of claiming such a toll?
I need not be a martyr or a mother, this I know,
to live in joy and confidence—my bail's been paid in full.

— Becca J. R. Lachman

FOR REFLECTION:

- This poem takes the structure of a hymn, a form of poetry that Christians throughout the ages have embraced.

- The hymn raises a series of questions. What chains are keeping you from experiencing the fullness of God's Spirit? What chains are you imposing on others?

- The image also draws our attention to themes of baptism. The Ethiopian became convicted of his need for baptism while reading a text from the Old Testament and hearing Philip's explication of that text. If you have been baptized what do you remember of the instruction that preceded that ritual?

- Married couples regularly celebrate anniversaries of their commitments. If you have made a baptismal commitment, how do you remember, or even celebrate, it? How do you keep the reality of your baptism alive? If you wrote a hymn about your baptism, what would it include?

ECONOMIC EQUALITY

READ: JAMES 2:1–13

My brothers and sisters, when you show favoritism you deny the faithfulness of our Lord Jesus Christ, who has been resurrected in glory. Imagine two people coming into your meeting. One has a gold ring and fine clothes, while the other is poor, dressed in filthy rags. Then suppose that you were to take special notice of the one wearing fine clothes, saying, "Here's an excellent place. Sit here." But to the poor person you say, "Stand over there"; or, "Here, sit at my feet." Wouldn't you have shown favoritism among yourselves and become evil-minded judges?

My dear brothers and sisters, listen! Hasn't God chosen those who are poor by worldly standards to be rich in terms of faith? Hasn't God chosen the poor as heirs of the kingdom he has promised to those who love him? But you have dishonored the poor. Don't the wealthy make life difficult for you? Aren't they the ones who drag you into court? Aren't they the ones who insult the good name spoken over you at your baptism?

You do well when you really fulfill the royal law found in scripture, *Love your neighbor as yourself.* But when you show favoritism, you are committing a sin, and by that same law you are exposed as a lawbreaker. Anyone who tries to keep all of the Law but fails at one point is guilty of failing to keep all of it. The one who said, *Don't commit adultery,* also said, *Don't commit murder.* So if you don't commit adultery but do commit murder, you are a lawbreaker. In every way, then, speak and act as people who will be judged by the law of freedom. There will be no mercy in judgment for anyone who hasn't shown mercy. Mercy overrules judgment.

Economic Equality SARAH FULLER

The Law of Liberty

You believe that God is one; you do well.
—James 2:19 (NRSVue)

Pay attention to what's torn,
the tears. The woman without
jewels. Without shoes.

Sit at my feet, you said.
Turn now, face one rich in faith.
Join hands. Let Mercy save you.

Rahab, border woman
on Jericho's wall, saved herself:
a pile of flax on the roof

hid God's strangers. Faith alone
without deeds is naught:
a flowing skirt of red chiffon.

—Raylene Hinz-Penner

FOR REFLECTION:

- The scripture passage from James is very specific in its expectation that followers of Jesus will not "show favoritism," especially to those who are wealthy. How would you react if these words were directed to your congregation or friendship circle?

- What do you think James means when he instructs his readers to "speak and act as people who will be judged by the law of freedom" (2:12)?

- This poem is short and compressed, sometimes using one-syllable words. Try writing a poem or prayer with one-syllable words. What do you notice?

ONE BODY IN CHRIST

READ: COLOSSIANS 3:1–17

Therefore, if you were raised with Christ, look for the things that are above where Christ is sitting at God's right side. Think about the things above and not things on earth. You died, and your life is hidden with Christ in God. When Christ, who is your life, is revealed, then you also will be revealed with him in glory.

So put to death the parts of your life that belong to the earth, such as sexual immorality, moral corruption, lust, evil desire, and greed (which is idolatry). The wrath of God is coming upon disobedient people because of these things. You used to live this way, when you were alive to these things. But now set aside these things, such as anger, rage, malice, slander, and obscene language. Don't lie to each other. Take off the old human nature with its practices and put on the new nature, which is renewed in knowledge by conforming to the image of the one who created it. In this image there is neither Greek nor Jew, circumcised nor uncircumcised, barbarian, Scythian, slave nor free, but Christ is all things and in all people.

Therefore, as God's choice, holy and loved, put on compassion, kindness, humility, gentleness, and patience. Be tolerant with each other and, if someone has a complaint against anyone, forgive each other. As the Lord forgave you, so also forgive each other. And over all these things put on love, which is the perfect bond of unity. The peace of Christ must control your hearts—a peace into which you were called in one body. And be thankful people. The word of Christ must live in you richly. Teach and warn each other with all wisdom by singing psalms, hymns, and spiritual songs. Sing to God with gratitude in your hearts. Whatever you do, whether in speech or action, do it all in the name of the Lord Jesus and give thanks to God the Father through him.

One Body in Christ RANDY HORST

One Body

Small miracles have started to occur
In what we'd thought of as a fallow field.
Birdsong and native lilies have returned;
As our dominion yields, the landscape heals.
Where just a year ago we had despaired
Of ever seeing them again, the bees,
With golden pollen coating every hair,
Dip eagerly into this floral sea.
Now slowly, painfully, we recognize
That we are of and not above creation,
That we are all fruits of the tree of life,
And we are called to live in right relation.
  We've seen diversity's a sign of love,
  And so we put on love and live as one.

—*Dennis Huffman*

FOR REFLECTION:

- This poem is a sonnet, structured in a traditional English (or Shakespearean) form. In English, sonnets tend to be written in iambic pentameter—that is, with a rhythmic beat in which each line (or iamb) contains five units (called feet) of unstressed and stressed syllables. English sonnets traditionally include fourteen lines, which follow a clear rhyming scheme and conclude with a couplet. Many sonnets, though certainly not all, focus on themes of love.

- The scripture passage explores what it means to be fully united to Christ—to live a life that is "hidden with Christ in God" (Colossians 3:3). Verses 12–17 paint a picture of what that might actually look like. Hold these verses in mind as you ponder the image and reflect on the poem. Where have you experienced "small miracles"?

PART 8

Visions of the Future

PRAISE THE LORD!

READ: PSALM 150

Praise the LORD!

Praise God in his sanctuary!
    Praise God in his fortress, the sky!
Praise God in his mighty acts!
    Praise God as suits his incredible greatness!
Praise God with the blast of the ram's horn!
    Praise God with lute and lyre!
Praise God with drum and dance!
    Praise God with strings and pipe!
Praise God with loud cymbals!
    Praise God with clashing cymbals!
Let every living thing praise the LORD!

Praise the LORD!

Praise the Lord! RANDY HORST

The Shape of Praise

Come open-handed to the sanctuary.
Park your heavy backpack,
empty your pockets, leave your sorrows
at the door.

A meadowlark is practicing
the scales of rejoicing. The west wind
whistles through the reeds and all the hills
clap their hands.

Your hands are shaped
to cradle instruments of peace. Strong fingers
rouse the harp strings. An open palm
summons a heart-beat from the drum.
Unclench your lips and blow
into the horn,

a warning:
the hungry are still with us
and the wounded.
Nations rage, the earth unfolds
her robes of mourning.

Your music rises
like smoke from sacrifice or forest fire.
Make it a prayer for mercy. A slender
shaft of gratitude.

—Sarah Klassen

FOR REFLECTION:

- "Let every living thing praise the LORD!" (Psalm 150:6). The psalmist imagines the possibility that praise to God extends beyond humans to "every living thing." Take some time to reflect on what that looks like. Consider writing a psalm of praise.

- What is your default mode of praising God? Why is music seemingly central to our expressions of praise?

- The poem takes a sudden turn in the fourth stanza when the horn becomes an instrument of warning. Ponder the relationship between praise and the reality of hunger, war, and those who wear "robes of mourning."

EZEKIEL'S FIRST VISION

READ: EZEKIEL 1:1–14

In the thirtieth year, on the fifth day of the fourth month, I was with the exiles at the Chebar River when the heavens opened and I saw visions of God. (It happened on the fifth day of the month, in the fifth year after King Jehoiachin's deportation. The LORD's word burst in on the priest Ezekiel, Buzi's son, in the land of Babylon at the Chebar River. There the LORD's power overcame him.)

As I watched, suddenly a driving storm came out of the north, a great cloud flashing fire, with brightness all around. At its center, in the middle of the fire, there was something like gleaming amber. And inside that were forms of four living creatures. This was what they looked like: Each had the form of a human being, though each had four faces and four wings. Their feet looked like proper feet, but the soles of their feet were like calves' hooves, and they shone like burnished bronze. Human hands were under their wings on all four sides. All four creatures had faces and wings, and their wings touched each other's wings. When they moved, they each went straight ahead without turning. As for the form of their faces: each of the four had a human face, with a lion's face on the right and a bull's face on the left, and also an eagle's face. The pairs of wings that stretched out overhead touched each other, while the other pairs covered their bodies. Each moved straight ahead wherever the wind propelled them; they moved without turning. Regarding the creatures' forms: they looked like blazing coals, like torches. Fire darted about between the creatures and illuminated them, and lightning flashed from the fire. The creatures looked like lightning streaking back and forth.

Ezekiel's First Vision MATTHEW REGIER

Divine Images

I

The windstorm spits sand in my eyes
as brilliant flashes of lightning open a glimpse
of four living creatures of fire:
Four wings enfold each creature,
each wing ending in a human hand.
Beside each being spins a wheel of topaz
rimmed with eyes. Within the wheel another wheel.
The wheels, infused with the spirit of being,
move wherever the creature moves.
Atop the wings of the four creatures rides
a gleaming figure who calls
my name. I fall to the ground.

II

How can I render Ezekiel's vision
in two dimensions? Millennia
before cinematography, he defies
the flatness of the page. Did his vision
come from ergot in the wheat,
or the timeless capacity of the mind
to layer image upon image,
to make something never seen
in heaven or on earth?

III

Where is the still, small voice?
The whisper? The intimate,
riding as a flea in the ear of lion or ox,
secreted in the tear duct of a disembodied eye,
encoded like DNA in an invisible cell?

IV

Sitting between my sister and my mother
on the long, curved pew, I learned
to fold and roll a handkerchief
to shape a baby in a cradle
in wordless instructions,
a gentle touch, while
the minister read
from Ezekiel.

—Ann Hostetler

FOR REFLECTION:

- For the full impact of this text, read the entire chapter—or for the really adventurous, read the first five chapters of Ezekiel.

- What are we to make of this vision, seemingly crafted, as the poet suggests, for "cinematographic" effect? What are your first responses as you absorb the visual images described in the text and so vividly depicted in the artwork?

- The poem reminds us of the various ways that people of faith encounter the divine. If you, like Ezekiel, were to claim the full range of your vocabulary and imagination, what words, metaphors, visions, or images would enable you to express a face-to-face encounter with God?

TREES OF LIVING WATER

READ: PSALM 1:1–3

The truly happy person
    doesn't follow wicked advice,
    doesn't stand on the road of sinners,
    and doesn't sit with the disrespectful.
Instead of doing those things,
    these persons love the LORD's Instruction,
    and they recite God's Instruction day and night!
They are like a tree replanted by streams of water,
    which bears fruit at just the right time
    and whose leaves don't fade.
        Whatever they do succeeds.

Trees of Living Water MATTHEW REGIER

You are like trees planted by streams of water

Walking to school through the park,
we watched for the day the ginkgos
lost all their leaves at once—
from tiny yellow fans on tender branches
to thousands underfoot, blowing across the grass,
a few tracked into schoolrooms
on the sides of wet autumn sneakers.

What if the nations dropped arms
like this?
All at once naked of all the guns?
It seems beyond impossible.
But then also how unlikely
is ginkgo's swift baring?
Abundant and vulnerable,
confident and strong.
Saying, Yes winter,
we are ready for the change.
What may look sudden
is no doubt the result
of millions of tiny signals sent
bark to branch, sap to stem.

So does the stream speak to the roots:
Keep going, we are flowing. You can weather
this season. We are strong.
Pass the message, through networks under duff:
Drop it all.

—*Sarah Kinsel*

FOR REFLECTION:

- Trees are powerful images throughout Scripture, as well as in the human experience generally. What biblical trees come to mind as you gaze at the artwork depicting this grove of trees?

- Let your mind wander to any various trees that have been significant to you at some point in your life. In the space below, tell the story of a specific tree. Describe its physical form. What key memories do you associate with this tree?

A SHOOT WILL GROW UP FROM THE STUMP OF JESSE

READ: ISAIAH 11:1–2, 6–9

A shoot will grow up from the stump of Jesse;
    a branch will sprout from his roots.
The LORD's spirit will rest upon him,
    a spirit of wisdom and understanding,
    a spirit of planning and strength,
    a spirit of knowledge and fear of the LORD.

. . . .

The wolf will live with the lamb,
    and the leopard will lie down with the young goat;
    the calf and the young lion will feed together,
    and a little child will lead them.
The cow and the bear will graze.
    Their young will lie down together,
    and a lion will eat straw like an ox.
A nursing child will play over the snake's hole;
    toddlers will reach right over the serpent's den.
They won't harm or destroy anywhere on my holy mountain.
    The earth will surely be filled with the knowledge of the LORD,
    just as the water covers the sea.

A Shoot Will Grow Up from the Stump of Jesse RANDY HORST

Fishing Jesse's Branch

Jesse's Branch broke
near the crest of the mountain,
a narrow stream of slanted rock
and water swimming with speckled
trout. From a small seep
chestnut stumps ghosted
the banks, a few shoots greening
before blight reminded them
their deaths arrived a hundred
years before. The first time
we read what Isaiah wrote
about the lamb and the leopard,
the lion and the goat, I was taken
with fear. Pastor Yoder teaches
the Scriptures are without error.
But everyone who lives
in these woods knows a bear
won't feed alongside a cow,
and lion's teeth can't grind straw.
In English class Mrs. Peachey told me
it's all metaphor. The earliest witnesses,
the Shawnee, long before we stole
their mountain, knew it as holy.
They say their Grandmother
made the world. I think we're
the wicked in their story.
After chores we play on talus
where timber rattlers den.
We're forbidden to pick them up,
although my friend James goes
to a church where they have enough
faith to handle them. His uncle
lost an arm after he was bitten.
I've thrown my line in a pool

that holds back Jesse's Branch,
slows the water where a fish might feed.
My eyes and ears hope for a rise
and its rings, for a splash at my back,
trout lifting in purple and orange.
When I cradle one in my hands,
the red dots on their sides
look just like God's eyes.

—*Todd Davis*

FOR REFLECTION:

- For many readers, it may be impossible to read the passage from Isaiah without thinking of the depictions of the "peaceable kingdom" by the Quaker minister and artist Edward Hicks. Randy Horst, the artist who created the accompanying image, engages the text in a very different way. What do you see in Horst's image that surprises you?

- In a similar way, the poem by Todd Davis unsettles the comfortable scene of the peaceable kingdom. He even suggests in the final line that nature, despite its cruelty, reveals something about God. How do you respond to this?

- Do you agree that the natural world, in the words of the poet Alfred, Lord Tennyson, is "red in tooth and claw"?

- Where do you find hope in the world of nature?

JOHN'S VISION: A WOMAN, HER CHILD, AND THE DRAGON

READ: REVELATION 12:1–6

Then a great sign appeared in heaven: a woman clothed with the sun, with the moon under her feet and a crown of twelve stars on her head. She was pregnant, and she cried out because she was in labor, in pain from giving birth. Then another sign appeared in heaven: it was a great fiery red dragon, with seven heads and ten horns, and seven royal crowns on his heads. His tail swept down a third of heaven's stars and threw them to the earth. The dragon stood in front of the woman who was about to give birth so that when she gave birth, he might devour her child. She gave birth to a son, a male child who is to rule all the nations with an iron rod. Her child was snatched up to God and his throne. Then the woman fled into the desert, where God has prepared a place for her. There she will be taken care of for one thousand two hundred sixty days.

John's Vision: A Woman, Her Child, and the Dragon RANDY HORST

Light from the Twelve Stars

First the wilderness with trees, a single-starred-mystery.
    Then a dragon—crocodilian, with seven
sovereign heads, ten horns, and seven gemmed diadems,

jaunty limbs at times leaden and lumbering. It could not
    see (with all its eyes) that despite its cruel intentions,
its crown-scissoring tail, emblazoned jaws ajar—light from

the twelve stars it split would clothe the earth and clothe
    a woman on the earth. (She fled to the wilderness
soon after giving birth.) Though only one she would not be

all alone. On a high dark branch a blackbird perched
    with its copse of cloaklike feathers, its prow-nibbed
beak, wings oiled with the magi's myrrh. A dragon

does not belong in the forest nor on Earth but only in
    story nor do the stars really (as crown) belong
but in the far-off sky. How else could her quiet knowing

be explained but through a language of light's own liking?
    Her baby was taken; she knew he would be—
not by the dragon though—when it (without circumspect),

within reach of the twelve took a third—it could not
    escape that light any more than she could escape
its fiery lizardry when she stood on the remnant planet,

a bright star behind it, the infant silent inside her womb.
    Crown-first we are all born here (into this
starry wilderness)—until that light cloth wraps us at birth.

(in memory of Don L. Troyer)

—Katie Lehman

FOR REFLECTION:

- Throughout the centuries, some readers have used the visions of John the Revelator as a Rosetta stone to reveal hidden meanings or to predict the imminent return of Christ. Others glance at these texts and, bewildered, turn elsewhere. The poem, by contrast, engages the images and reframes them, leaving us with a sense of wonder—"Crown-first we are all born here (into this / starry wilderness)—until that light cloth wraps us at birth."

- Spend some time allowing the images from the text, the poem, and the artwork to dance in your mind. What lingers with you? What thought or action is about to be born in you? Consider writing a poem or a prayer.

SCRIPTURE INDEX

THE ARTISTS

SARAH FULLER is a Canadian artist living in Ventura, California. She participates in both the Catholic Worker movement and the Mennonite church. She is inspired by religious icons, botanical prints, folk art, liturgical art, and illustrations produced for the *Catholic Worker* newspaper. She is interested in fostering community through art making.

RANDY HORST is a graduate of Hesston College, Goshen College, and Bowling Green State University. He taught art, art history, and graphic design for thirty-three years in Ohio, Montana, and Indiana, with the final thirteen years at Goshen College. Now retired, he lives in Goshen making art and music.

LISA OBIREK is an artist and mother from Treaty One land in Winnipeg, Manitoba, where she has lived, worked, and learned at the intersections of social services and the arts for two decades—and, she hopes, for many more decades to come.

DONA PARK is a Korean Canadian living in Abbotsford, British Columbia. She grew up living in both Canada and the United States, with international experiences scattered in between. Her artwork often touches on the reality of existing between transient spaces and cross-cultural experiences, immigration, and womanhood through a variety of media.

MATTHEW REGIER is an artist, community organizer, and pastor. Matthew and his wife Tia Regier cofounded The School for Rural Culture and Creativity in Matfield Green, Kansas, where they live with their two children.

THE POETS

JULIA BAKER lives on the coast of Maine, where she engages beauty and brokenness through words on the page, watercolor flow, and hospital chaplaincy.

KIRSTEN EVE BEACHY lives in the Shenandoah Valley of Virginia and works at Eastern Mennonite University. She writes and thinks about backyard poultry, Mennonite martyrs, caretaking, infertility, and disability. Her in-progress book shares her confessions as a "granola" Mennonite.

CONNIE T. BRAUN is an author and poet from Vancouver, British Columbia. Connie's poetry appears in anthologies, journals, and is set to musical composition, with a collection forthcoming from CMU Press. Braun is honored to contribute to this endeavor, and to other works and organizations centered on peace.

ABIGAIL CARL-KLASSEN is a writer, researcher, poet, educator, translator, and activist living in El Paso, Texas. Her poetry collection, *Village Mechanics*, is forthcoming from FlowerSong Press, and recordings of her oral history project, "Rebels, Exiles, and Bridge Builders: Cross-Cultural Encounters in the Campos Menonitas of Chihuahua," can be found on the Darp Stories YouTube channel.

TODD DAVIS is the author of eight books of poetry, most recently *Ditch Memory: New & Selected Poems*, published by Michigan State University Press. He is an emeritus fellow of the Black Earth Institute and a professor of environmental studies at Pennsylvania State University's Altoona College. A member of University Mennonite Church, he hunts and fishes along the Allegheny Front near his home in Tipton, Pennsylvania.

CHERYL DENISE has roots in Elmira, Ontario. She now lives in West Virginia with her husband Mike Miller in a timber frame home they built themselves. She is the author of the poetry books *Fences*, *What's in the Blood*, and *I Saw God Dancing*, all published by Cascadia Publishing House.

PATRICK FRIESEN lives in Victoria, Canada, and has published poetry, essays, co-translations with Per Brask, and stage and radio plays. He has collaborated on two music/spoken word albums with Niko Friesen. Most recently he published *Reckoning* with Anvil and recorded an album of spoken word. Website: PatrickFriesen.com.

JOSEPH GASCHO is a retired cardiologist, poet, and photographer. In addition to poetry books about his growing-up years in rural Nebraska and his cardiology career, he's published two books related to the liturgical year: *Lent Then and Now: People, Poems, and Portraits* and *Advent Then and Now: People, Poems, and Portraits.*

CHARITY GINGERICH teaches, writes, and sings from her little yellow barn office (within earshot of Almanzo the rooster, who is an aspiring operatic tenor). She enjoys singing with various choral groups. You can find her first full collection of poems, *After June* (Green Writers Press, 2019), wherever books are sold.

DEBRA GINGERICH lives in Sarasota, Florida, with her husband and dog. She has an MFA in writing from Vermont College and has published a collection of poetry titled *Where We Start.*

JEFF GUNDY is completing a term as writer in (non)residence at Bluffton University after decades of teaching there. His thirteen books include *Without a Plea* (poems), *Wind Farm: Landscape with Stories and Towers* (nonfiction), and *Songs from an Empty Cage: Poetry, Mystery, Anabaptism, and Peace.* He still really wants to be a singer-songwriter and recently bought a mandolin.

RAYLENE HINZ-PENNER is a lifelong Kansan and retired college English teacher at Bethel College and Washburn University who writes about the land (*Searching for Sacred Ground: The Journey of Chief Lawrence Hart* and *East of Liberal: Notes on the Land*). She is passionate about work to dismantle the Doctrine of Discovery and for Indigenous justice.

ANITA HOOLEY YODER is a campus minister, teacher, and theopoet. She lives near Cleveland, Ohio, with her husband Ben and attends Friendship Mennonite Church. She loves good books, good food, and bad Cleveland sports teams.

CARMEN SUSANA HORST lives in Goshen, Indiana, with her spouse and two teenage daughters. She is a spiritual director, Mennonite pastor, and former doula. She enjoys words and the silence between them, drinking maté tea, and her daughters' humor.

ANN HOSTETLER is the author of two books of poems, *Safehold* and *Empty Room with Light*, as well as the editor of *A Cappella: Mennonite Voices in Poetry*. She is also the editor of the online *Journal of Mennonite Writing* at MennoniteWriting.org. She taught English and creative writing for twenty-two years at Goshen College, where she is now professor emerita. Her poems and scholarly essays have appeared in numerous journals and anthologies.

SHERI HOSTETLER has been on the pastoral team at First Mennonite Church of San Francisco since 2000. She is also the cofounder of the Coalition to Dismantle the Doctrine of Discovery. She is trained as a spiritual director and a permaculturist and lives on an island in San Francisco Bay.

DENNIS HUFFMAN grew up on an apple farm in northeastern Ohio and graduated from Goshen College in 1980. Since retiring from Prince George's Community College, he's published a book of poems and photos about invasive plants in the parks around Takoma Park, Maryland, where he lives with his wife Susan.

JEAN JANZEN grew up as the seventh child in a family of preachers, teachers, and musicians, where the power of words was a lively element in the home. Entering that world of words with poetry in midlife, now into old age, has been a fertile and joyous journey. Janzen lives in Fresno, California.

CARITA KEIM lives in Holmes County, Ohio. She's worked as an educator in K–12 schools and the museum Behalt. Fostering authentic communication between people is her lifework. Like many contributors to this book, she likes to read, hike, and learn new things.

SARAH KINSEL lives at the eastern edge of Portland, Oregon, in the Johnson Creek watershed, where she writes, parents, pastors, and spends time with Douglas fir, cedar, and dogwood. She is ordained in the Church of the Brethren.

SARAH KLASSEN reads and writes in Winnipeg, where she taught high school English and writes fiction and poetry. A "New & Selected" volume of her poems was released in 2024.

BECCA J. R. LACHMAN works in the land of public libraries in Appalachian Ohio. Her poetry collections include *What I say to this house*, *The Apple Speaks*, and *Other Acreage*. She is also the editor of *A Ritual to Read Together*, a national anthology that marked the centennial of the late poet and conscientious objector William Stafford. A member of Columbus Mennonite Church, Becca has contributed lyrics to the *Voices Together* hymnal ("Could It Be That God Is Singing?") and has been a featured guest artist at Mennonite Arts Weekend in Cincinnati, Ohio. She lives in Athens, Ohio, with her husband and daughter.

KATIE LEHMAN received a BA in English from Goshen College in 1995 and an MFA in creative writing from the University of Notre Dame in 1999. From 2004 to 2010, Lehman was assistant editor at the University of Notre Dame Press. She is the volume editor of John Matthias's *Regrounding a Pilgrimage* (Dos Madres, 2018). Her poetry collection *Emily Dickinson's Lexicon* was published by Dos Madres in 2023. Lehman is the associate editor of the UK-based journal *The Fortnightly Review*.

OBI MARTIN is a communitarian living on the west side of Pittsburgh, where he rotates among teaching, gardening, renovating, offering hospitality, and sitting still. You can read more of his work at TheCurator.org, where he is a contributing editor.

SHANNON MCKEEHEN, author of *Barbra in Shadow* and *Just a Trick of the Light*, is a Quaker, poet, and educator who received her MFA in creative writing from Mills College and doctorate in composition from Kent State University. She lives in Ohio with her husband and cats.

RUTH ANN MEYERS KULP has been a professional singer, voice teacher, and music therapist. She explores questions and emotions through music, art, and poetry. Her poems have appeared in *Ekphrasis Poetry Journal*, *The Other Side*, *Cicada*, and others. Her recent poetry chapbook, *An Angle of Grace*, was published by The Orchard Street Press.

JESSE NATHAN was raised in northern California and rural Kansas and attended both San Francisco Mennonite Church and his mother's home community of Eden

Mennonite. His first book of poems, *Eggtooth*, won the 2024 New Writers Award in Poetry. Nathan teaches literature at the University of California, Berkeley. He lives in Oakland.

RUTH NAYLOR, a Bluffton College graduate and member of Bluffton's First Mennonite Church, has published two books of poetry, *A Family Affair* and *Straw & All*, plus *Faith Talk: A Spiritual Memoir Inviting Reflection and Dialogue*. A variety of well over sixty different publications have included her poetry or prose.

BARBARA NICKEL grew up in Saskatchewan and now lives and writes in Yarrow, British Columbia, on the Stó:lō territory of the Pilalt and Ts'elxwéyeqw. Her most recent poetry collection is *Essential Tremor*. Her work has appeared in many publications, including *Best Canadian Poetry 2021*, *The Walrus*, and *Best Canadian Poetry 2024*.

LEONARD NOLT graduated from Amarillo College and Boise State University. He's had photos and writings published since the 1960s. He recently self-published a book of poems entitled *The End of a Day*. Nolt has served on the board of the Pacific Northwest Mennonite Conference, is a retired respiratory therapist, and lives in Idaho.

KEITH RATZLAFF is professor emeritus of English at Central College in Pella, Iowa, where he lives. He's been awarded two Pushcart Prizes and has been included in *The Best American Poetry*. He's a die-hard fan of the Chicago Cubs.

ANGELINE SCHELLENBERG is a contemplative spiritual director, photographer, mudlarker, and the author of *Tell Them It Was Mozart*, *Fields of Light and Stone*, and *Mondegreen Riffs*. She copyedited the *MB Herald* (2010–2019) and attends Imago Dei Christian Community in Winnipeg, where she lives with her husband, adult children, and dog.

DANIEL SHANK CRUZ (they/multitudes) is a queer disabled boricua who grew up in the Bronx and Lancaster, Pennsylvania. Multitudes is the author of a book of literary criticism, *Queering Mennonite Literature* (2019), and a hybrid memoir/literary critical text, *Ethics for Apocalyptic Times* (2024), both published by Penn State University Press.

JESSICA SMUCKER's writings have appeared in *Spoon River Poetry Review*, *Potomac Review*, *Hawai'i Review*, *The Dirty Goat*, *The Mennonite*, *MennoNot*, *Turnrow*, *CMW*

Journal, Vision: A Journal for Church and Theology, A Cappella: Mennonite Voices in Poetry, and elsewhere. She is also a nationally touring singer-songwriter with several produced albums of original songs. She lives in Lancaster, Pennsylvania.

ESTHER YODER STENSON lives with her husband David in Harrisonburg, Virginia, where she attends Community Mennonite Church. She enjoys walking in wild places, watching birds, growing vegetables, and writing. She has published two collections of poetry, *Miracle Temple* and *Showing Up*, and a memoir, *Doors through the Great Wall.*

JULIE SWARSTAD JOHNSON is a poet who lives in Tucson, Arizona, where she works as an archivist and librarian. Her book *Orchard Light* (2020) considers—through poems—the experiences of Christian pacifists during the American Civil War. She is currently finishing a collection of poems focused on the night sky.

ADAM M. L. TICE is a hymn writer and editor. He is a Fellow of The Hymn Society and a recipient of Goshen College's Culture for Service Award. He resides in Goshen, Indiana, with his spouse María and son Ezra.

SHARI MILLER WAGNER is a former Indiana Poet Laureate (2016–2017) and the author of three books of poems: *The Farm Wife's Almanac, The Harmonist at Nightfall,* and *Evening Chore.* She lives in Westfield, Indiana, and is currently writing poems about the Indiana dunes and people from Indiana history.

DAVID WALTNER-TOEWS has published more than twenty books of poetry, fiction, and science. His work integrates family and Anabaptist history, the nature of love, zoonoses, pandemics, ecology, health, and excrement. He is an Officer of the Order of Canada, which cited him "for his leadership and expertise in ecosystem approaches to health, and for supporting development worldwide." He lives on land that is the traditional home of the Haudenosaunee, Anishinaabe, and Neutral People.

DAVID C. WRIGHT is a professor of English at Monmouth College. He is the author of several poetry collections, including *A Liturgy for Stones* and *The Small Books of Bach.* Several of his hymn texts also appear in *Voices Together.*

THE EDITORS

EILEEN R. KINCH is digital editor at *Anabaptist World.* She studied English at Chatham College and writing as ministry at Earlham School of Religion. She is the author of *Gathering the Silence* (Finishing Line Press). Her poetry has appeared in various journals and anthologies, including *Foreshadow, Topology Magazine, Convivium, Fledgling Rag,* and *Enlivened by the Mystery: Quakers and God.* Her essays have appeared in the *Journal of Mennonite Writing, CrossCurrents,* and the *Mezzo Cammin* Women Poets Timeline. She and her husband Joel Nofziger live near Tylersport, Pennsylvania, with their two cats. She is a member of Keystone Friends Meeting in Lancaster County.

JOHN D. ROTH is project director of MennoMedia's Anabaptism at 500 initiative. Prior to that role, Roth was a professor of history at Goshen College (1985–2022), where he also served as director of the Mennonite Historical Library and editor of the *Mennonite Quarterly Review.* Roth has published widely on topics related to Anabaptist-Mennonite history, theology, and church life. He is also the founding director of the Institute for the Study of Global Anabaptism at Goshen College and is active in Mennonite World Conference. John and his wife Ruth enjoy spending time with their grandchildren and are members of Berkey Avenue Mennonite Fellowship in Goshen, Indiana.

WONDERINGS & WANDERINGS

WONDERINGS & WANDERINGS

WONDERINGS & WANDERINGS

WONDERINGS & WANDERINGS

WONDERINGS & WANDERINGS

WONDERINGS & WANDERINGS

WONDERINGS & WANDERINGS